The Play of Gilgamesh

EDWIN MORGAN was born in Glasgow in 1920. He became lecturer in English at the University of Glasgow, from which he retired as Professor in 1980. He was appointed Poet Laureate of Glasgow in 1999, and received the Queen's Gold Medal for Poetry in 2000. In June 2001 he received the Weidenfeld Prize for Translation for *Phaedra*. In 2004 Edwin Morgan was appointed Scotland's Makar, or Poet Laureate.

T0169311

EDWIN MORGAN

The Play of Gilgamesh

CARCANET

Acknowledgements

Parts of this play have previously appeared in the following magazines:
Interchange, *Metre*, *Poetry Ireland Review*, *Scotia Review*, *PN Review*.

First published in Great Britain in 2005 by
Carcanet Press Limited
Alliance House
Cross Street
Manchester M2 7AQ

A CIP catalogue record for this book is available from the British Library
ISBN 1 85754 841 8

The publisher acknowledges financial assistance from Arts Council England

Typeset by XL Publishing Services, Tiverton
Printed and bound in England by SRP Ltd, Exeter

Introduction

Gilgamesh is the hero of an ancient poem, and a large part of the story concerns his personal quest, told through a series of adventures of great interest and strangeness. Unlike Beowulf or King Arthur, Gilgamesh is a well-attested historical figure who ruled the kingdom of Sumer in what is now southern Iraq around 2700 BC. But like these other two heroes, he became the focus for many legends and mythical extensions which took his story well beyond the realities of third-millennium Iraq. Tales and rumours about his deeds began to circulate in Sumerian literature not long after his death. How far they were orally transmitted we cannot be sure, but they were certainly written down, as literate poetry, and the Sumerians prided themselves on the importance of recording, probably because they regarded themselves (rightly, as far as we know) as the originators of the earliest complete writing system, sometime in the fourth millennium: the writing we know as cuneiform, a wedge-shaped script made by pressing a reed stylus into clay. Their own language, which has no known relatives, died out and was replaced by Akkadian, a Semitic language, but the Akkadians (or Babylonians, as they are sometimes called), who admired and respected Sumerian culture, copied and translated and re-edited the Sumerian poems, including the epic of Gilgamesh. Though their language was quite different, they still used the cuneiform script and clay tablets, and if it were not for these sun-baked tablets dug up in Iraq and other parts of the Middle East we would know nothing about Gilgamesh. It was touch and go in any case, since knowledge of the cuneiform script was lost about the time of Christ, and the whole Gilgamesh story disappeared for nearly two millennia, until after the writing was deciphered in the middle of the nineteenth century. The Hebrews, Greeks and Romans did not refer to Gilgamesh, and so his legend never passed into the mainstream of Western culture, which is a great pity, as his story is a remarkable one. We have made amends to some extent in recent times, with dramatic and novelised versions, and with an opera/oratorio by the Slovak composer Martinů. In the days of the American Beat poets, Gregory Corso read a translation in prison and was so greatly struck by it that he learned most of it by heart, and later said he 'couldn't work with anyone who didn't know it'. The poem's power can still be felt after five thousand years, a fact all the more striking when you consider that there are gaps in the text where tablets have been damaged or are missing, and that there are still some words whose meaning is uncertain or unknown.

My own involvement with Gilgamesh came out of being asked to write a play for the Communicado Theatre Company in Edinburgh, with whom I had worked before. (Eventually the company broke up, and the play was not performed.) I thought the story had good dramatic potential if given the right treatment, so I wrote my version, as a poetic play with metre and rhyme, keeping close to the plot but developing some of the characters, introducing one or two new ones, and writing a few bridge scenes where the original was obscure or disjointed. I also wrote in some songs, which gave a sort of Brechtian comment on the action. So I had my own quest for this questing hero, and the more I studied the poem the more interesting he became: a great man certainly, in the historical sense, builder of cities, defender of a powerful and wealthy state, encourager of all the arts and crafts, yet a complex figure with marked flaws, moody, overbearing, at times impatient, at times indulgent and generous, emotionally swinging between elation and black depression. He is young, handsome, strong, unmarried. What do the gods have in store for him? You might think they would want to make him a tragic hero, give him a memorable death. But in fact this does not happen, and Gilgamesh returns after many adventures to his native city of Uruk, chastened by sufferings and disappointments, a more humanly sympathetic figure. The poem ends as it had begun, praising the strength and beauty of the great walled city which is Gilgamesh's monument. So the epic is in celebration of a man and a city, but it also asks questions about both. What lasts, what changes, what survives? Is anything immortal? To get any real answers we have to – Gilgamesh has to – go outside the city, into the world of nature, into the wasteland where the quest can take place.

The story begins by showing the more problematic side of the hero. The populace are restive under his arrogance and high-handedness, especially his habit of having young men and women lifted off the street and 'disappearing' – no one knows what he wants them for – or what happens to them – and the poem does not say either, which makes it all the more ominous and sinister. A group of citizens decides to do something about it, their plot being to bring forward a rival to the king, someone of equal force who would curb his wilfulness, make him think twice about his anti-social actions. They pick on someone who in fact is going to change the whole course of Gilgamesh's life. Enkidu is a wild man, a 'green man', a child of nature, living in the woods outside the city, untamed, friendly with the animals, almost like an animal himself with thick body hair, keen senses, great physical strength. They lure him into the city by means of a sacred harlot from the Temple of Ishtar. She goes out into the countryside and overcomes his shyness by (as the poem says) 'loosening her dress and exposing her sex', and Enkidu lies with her in a state of constant arousal 'for six days and seven nights'. The harlot brings him back to the city, but now that he is tainted with the smell of human intercourse his animal friends desert him, and he regrets this – though obviously he still retains enough natural strangeness to work as a counter-balance to the perhaps over-civilised urban culture of Uruk. There is a great buzz of interest as Enkidu is brought into the market-place, and sits down to his first urban meal: the harlot, Shamhat, plies him with venison and beer, after he has been living off nuts and spring water, and he becomes slightly drunk and loquacious:

I tell you – Shamhat – friends – Uruk citizens –
the forest is a wonderful place, and its denizens –
now there's a word I like, they live in dens
the ones I love – are no longer mine, or men's,
but only nature's. I, she, we broke the link.
I've eaten flesh, and water's not my drink.
But I must say this drink is very very –
I do feel different – it's extraordinary –
the woods, the lions, doves, gazelles are fading –
no more panting, pawing, purring, parading –
scents of Shamhat have killed the fetid pelts
I used to mingle sweat with – buckles and belts
are good to feel instead of ivies and snakes –
I never thought I'd think so – see these cakes,
these cakes, I don't know who made them, but
they're absolutely – picture me gnawing a nut
a week ago under a walnut tree
and calling it a banquet – now I'm free,
I'm free, my friends, the green world and the red
meet in my veins and here you see a head
that swings all round Uruk and smells misgivings.
I have come to change the nature of things.
(*He bangs tankard on table*)
Where's Gilgamesh?

Enkidu does not have long to wait. There is a wedding procession in the square, and as it emerges Gilgamesh sweeps in with his retinue and demands the bride for the first night as his *droit du seigneur*. But Enkidu steps forward and bars his way, tells him there is going to be no more *droit du seigneur*, he has come to change the order of things. Gilgamesh is amazed and angry, but impressed by the size and looks of the wild man. He proposes a wrestling-match, which takes place after they have stripped off. They are evenly matched, but Gilgamesh wins, perhaps because Enkidu has been drinking too much and has also been weakened by his seven nights of love. They break, respecting each other, and vow to become friends, so much so in fact that eventually Enkidu sits on a throne beside Gilgamesh, more like a second king than a trusted servant. This friendship between the two men is the backbone of the poem, and the author, whoever he was, pulls out all the stops to make us understand the depth and intensity of the relationship. The word 'love' is used; even the word 'bride' is used. Does this mean that it is not only the oldest poem in the world but the oldest gay poem in the world? That would be a matter of definition. Both Gilgamesh and Enkidu have sex with women, but they are in love only with each other. Whether there was anything physical in that love, the poem does not make clear, though it appears to drop several hints, from the erotic symbolism of the naked wrestling-match to Gilgamesh's later dreams of making two discoveries, first of something fallen from heaven like a meteorite, and then of a large man-sized axe, both of which he wrestles with, lifts, embraces, kisses, and virtually makes love to. His mother interprets both dreams as applying to Enkidu. But whatever we read into these episodes, the main point in the plot at this stage is that Enkidu sees it as his mission to moderate Gilgamesh's authoritarian behaviour and make him a better ruler, and he is beginning to make some progress in this when the plot takes a new turn and becomes a triangle situation. This comes about after the two men come back from a dangerous adventure into the mountains and cedars of Lebanon to bring back a supply of cedarwood for the great but shaky gates of Uruk. In the course of doing this they kill the monster Humbaba who is the official guardian of the cedar forest. This joint action brings them even closer together but displeases the gods, since it was wrong for Enkidu, a wild man, to destroy the wild guardian demon of the forest, and this has bad consequences later on. But in the meantime, once the two heroes have returned in triumph to Uruk with their cedarwood, to public acclaim, the high priestess Ishtar, centre of a love cult, casts her eye on Gilgamesh and thinks it would be nice to have him and to become his queen. So she does her best to drive a wedge between Gilgamesh and Enkidu, and makes a spectacular but clearly doomed offer to marry Gilgamesh, who is not the marrying kind. There is a splendid scene of black comedy where he rejects her advances with a counter-attack on her reputation as a nocturnal nymphomaniac. She may have power and wealth, he says, but she is no better than she should be. Gilgamesh may well be right, but we have no way of judging. The way he treats her is a clear example of what the Greeks were to call *hubris*, and both he and Enkidu were now wide open to the displeasure of the gods. After a total public humiliation, Ishtar vows revenge and appeals to the gods for it. She asks for the Bull of Heaven to come and ravage the city. The gods reluctantly agree; the Bull comes down; but Gilgamesh and Enkidu fight it and kill it. If anything they are even more self-confident and arrogant than before. The sky-god Anu and the sun-god Shamash meet and decide that something must be done about them. One of them must die. After much argument they say it will be Enkidu, who has committed the greater sin, as a renegade who killed the guardian of the cedar forest.

From that moment, Enkidu falls sick from a mysterious wasting disease which the royal doctors have not seen before and which they cannot cure. After a couple of feverish weeks in bed, he dies, in despair at such an unheroic death, and having told Gilgamesh his ominous dream of the afterlife (one of the finest passages in the poem): a demon, part man, part lion, part eagle, takes him away:

He then prepared me for another sphere.
He feathered my arms like wings, he gripped me tight,

he led me down into the House of Night,
the House where those who enter do not come out,
the road of no return winds them about,
the House where those who live there have no light,
eat clay, sup mud, and though there is no flight
are clothed with feathers, stalking round like birds,
looking for the no light they stalk towards.
The door and the lock of that House are dust-encrusted.
It is the House of Dust, where zombies are mustered.
All round I saw piles of crowns like skulls.
All round I heard dead kings like kitchen trulls
shuffle to serve the gods with meats and sweetmeats
or pour thin skins of water at their seats.
In the House of Dust I saw where the high priest sits
with acolytes, exorcists, evangelists
and all the anointed priests of the pantheon.
I saw Ereshkigal, Underworld Queen,
seated there with Beletseri, Underworld Scribe,
kneeling before her and reading out the tribe
of the dying and the dead. She lifted up her head
when she saw me. 'Who brought him?' she said.

Gilgamesh is totally distraught by Enkidu's death. He tears his robe from top to bottom, refuses all solace, goes about unkempt, and eventually tells his mother (who is very close to him in the poem) that he cannot go on living in Uruk. If a young vigorous healthy man like Enkidu can die, not by an enemy's sword but by some unseen virus in the blood, no one is safe; he too might die young, might die tomorrow; what use would his kingdom be then? What is life for, if you are going to be cut off in your twenties or thirties? No sooner had he gained a friend, a companion, a helper, a conscience, than this was swept away. Death was the enemy. How could he defeat death? The remainder of the poem describes his quest for immortality. He tells his mother – she tries unsuccessfully to dissuade him – that he will become an exile, a wanderer, a pilgrim, he will put on rough skins and go out half-naked into the wasteland in search of immortal life. He has heard that there is in the world, in some distant land, one immortal person, and he must find him and wrest his secret from him. This person is called Ziusura, Ziusura the Faraway, evidently the original of the biblical Noah, though unlike Noah he was granted not only survival but immortality. So Gilgamesh strips himself of all his royalty, dresses himself in animal skins (an interesting backward tribute to Enkidu), takes a staff and a knapsack, puts a dagger and an axe in his belt, and wanders off into the wilderness. Before he goes he orders his best sculptors and artificers to make and erect a huge statue of Enkidu, in gold and lapis-lazuli, as a permanent memorial.

His quest takes him through a series of bizarre and dangerous adventures which are shown to be tests and challenges, challenges to see whether he is really serious and determined in his search. He meets a Scorpion-Man and his mate a Scorpion-Woman who rattle and scuttle and hiss at him and do their best to scare him off, but he persuades them to let him pass. He moves into mountainous country, and is assailed at night by howling noises, and buffeted by gusts of wind and by the whirring wings of half-seen birds. He comes to the coast, where there is a tavern by the edge of the sea, guarded by a very robust and suspicious female innkeeper called Siduri. She says the pub is closed, and if he has come to rob her she will put up a good fight and has a fierce dog to help her. Gilgamesh is in rags by this time, dusty and generally filthy; she laughs at him when he tells her he is a king. However, he takes off his gold ring with the royal seal and asks her to examine it, and she is – almost – convinced. He goes on to describe his quest, and his earnestness and eloquence at last win her over and she agrees to help him. This is what he says:

> Tavern-keeper, the flower
> of youth, my friend and brother Enkidu,
> sharer of many dangers we came through,
> co-striker at Humbaba and the Bull,
> my friend who shared all hardship to the full
> and whom I deeply love, Enkidu who
> shared all that hardship to the full, who knew
> I deeply loved him, has served the general fate
> of men. I mourned him, desolate,
> letting no one bury him till the worm
> crawled from his nose. I was unclean, infirm,
> terrified, dying! I would follow him,
> how could I escape? The worm was so grim,
> the face was so dreadful, I tore my robes,
> I cried, I began to roam long roads.
> How could I be silent, how could I be still?
> He is clay, the friend I love. What skill,
> what search, what secret can save me from the clay?

It turns out that this is his first real breakthrough. Siduri has heard of Ziusura the Faraway, knows where he lives, across trackless seas and the Waters of the Dead, and if Gilgamesh wants to take the risk, there is a ferryman who will help him. She points out the ferryman, and Gilgamesh goes to meet him and explain what he wants. This is another edgy encounter, though the king and the ferryman eventually become good friends. Gilgamesh is in one of his moods, and when he hears that the boat is propelled by some sort of lodestones, magnetic stones, he does not like this idea. He takes his axe and smashes the stones, to the fury of the ferryman, a spirited young man called Urshanabi, who says to him:

> Gilgamesh, we now have an engineless ferry,
> do you hear me, a non-magnetic wherry.
> It suits the job: here is a king in tatters,
> itching to broach improbably high matters
> with my improbable master, Ziusura.
> There isn't any chapter, verse, or sura
> I'm sure he couldn't quote and say 'Discuss!'
> He is the Faraway, but he draws us
> even without a lodestone. Are we strong then?
> What are we in the field and lot of men?
> If you are not afraid to be a wood-cutter
> once more, we'll make some oars to get this cutter
> going – oars, punt-poles, masts, whatever,
> for deeps or shallows, doldrums or wild weather.
> You could be fishing for a final cast!
> The lubber king will serve before the mast
> or even be the mast! Go take your axe,
> cut down some young and springy trees; quick hacks,
> rough work will do; time presses; then to the boat.

Gilgamesh, perhaps impressed by this brisk young chap, obediently goes to the wood and brings back the necessary oars and poles, and they set off into the open sea. After days of voyaging, they come to the Waters of the Dead. They need a sail to cross this, so Gilgamesh, as the ferryman had prophesied, has to strip off his animal skin, buckle himself to one of the poles to make a mast, and spread out the pelt with his arms to make a sail and catch the wind – a strange scene, with a mixture of the humiliating (the ferryman carefully watching the naked king to see that he does everything right) and the heroic (the king becoming almost the spirit of the boat, driving it successfully to shore).

So they land in Ziusura's country. Urshanabi secures the boat while Gilgamesh puts on his pelt again. A man comes forward and politely challenges the king to say who he is and what is his business. This is in fact Ziusura, though Gilgamesh does not know it yet. He had expected that the immortal Ziusura would look the part, a sort of Swiftian Struldbrug with the wrinkles of hundreds or thousands of years, but the truth was that the gods, when they gave Ziusura and his family immortal life, allowed them to retain the age they had at the time of the Flood. All this the king learns later on. In the meantime he explains his mission, his grief at the death of his friend and his search for the secret of immortality. Ziusura chides him for not accepting that death is natural, and for harping on his own suffering when plenty of other people are perhaps suffering more. Gilgamesh cries out: 'My need is terrible. I am broken. I need life.' But Ziusura replies:

> We all need life, but then there comes a knife.
> We need a life, but then we get a death.
> It stalks us with its old insidious breath.
> No one can see it, no one sees its face.
> Its savage grimace has no shape, no grace.
> How long do we think home and hearth will last?
> How long will the sealed document be passed?
> How long do brothers share their inheritance?
> How long will rivers rise and swell to the dance
> of dragonflies with their eyes turned to the sun?
> But no one really sees the sun, not one.
> The sleeping and the dead are but as pictures,
> but death is not a picture; divine strictures
> make dreadful secrets better secret. The day
> of its coming, even to Ziusura the Faraway,
> is hidden.

At this, Gilgamesh realises that he is talking to the man he has been searching for. 'You are Ziusura, are you not?' he asks. And Ziusura replies, 'I am.' The impressive imagery of Ziusura's poetry and philosophy reminds us once again what a sophisticated poem this is, not at all primitive despite its early date, and probably with a tradition of lost poetry behind it, back into the fourth millennium. After these initial exchanges, Ziusura invites Gilgamesh into his house, where his wife prepares them a meal, with some good wine, and they talk about various things, but always circling back to the theme of survival, of human life and death. Ziusura decides to tell his story, as Gilgamesh had told his. This is the story of the Flood, very similar to the account in the book of Genesis, except that the Sumerian gods are divided about the rightness of destroying what they have created, and there is some angry discussion as to whether anyone should be saved. The Flood does go ahead, however, and one family builds an ark which eventually comes to rest on a mountain-top as the waters recede; this family is saved, and is given everlasting life. The poem presents the Flood itself with great vividness, all the more so because it is told in the first person by Ziusura, who was there; his memory is sharp even after thousands of years.

Following this account of how Ziusura became immortal, Gilgamesh feels it is time to revert to his own quest, and he asks directly if he can be given the secret of how he can defeat death. But Ziusura has to test him first, to see if he deserves it. He has to sit against the wall with his head between his knees, not moving at all or lying down, or sleeping, the whole night through. Poor Gilgamesh does his best, but the combination of tiredness after the journey, and the wine he has drunk, beats him, and he falls asleep. Ziusura and his wife watch him closely, but he remains sound asleep. Eventually Ziusura shakes him awake, and mocks him:

> Gilgamesh, where have you been?
> Eternal life has come and gone unseen.
> Where is the lion, the great hunter, now?
> Where are the conscious lightnings of his brow?
> I cannot help you; you have failed the test.
> You must go back; to go homewards is best.

Gilgamesh is in total misery, as all his hopes seem to have crashed:

> Oh Ziusura, what is to become of me?
> What shall I do, by either land or sea?
> The Raptor has sunk his claws into my flesh.
> Death has squatted in the rooms of Gilgamesh.
> Wherever I go, there already is Death!

But Ziusura is immovable. He gives Gilgamesh new clothes which he says will never soil, and he tells Urshanabi the ferryman to take the king back to Uruk. Gilgamesh is washed and oiled and dressed in his new robes, and is about to set off with the ferryman when Ziusura's wife, a kindly soul who had taken pity on him, persuades her husband to at least give the king *something* to take back home. Ziusura tells him to pluck a special plant which has the power not to confer eternal life but to rejuvenate ageing tissues. Gilgamesh does this, and he and the ferryman go off with the plant, travelling back not by sea this time but by a long overland trek.

The men are in relatively good spirits, since they are not returning empty-handed. Somewhere en route they make camp for the night in a forest glade. They lay down their packs, and Gilgamesh carefully lays down the medicinal plant. Then they go off to gather brushwood for a fire. When they come back with the brushwood they are just in time to see a large snake slither out of the trees, snatch the plant in its jaws, and go back into the undergrowth. Before it disappears, it sloughs its skin, to show a shining new body. The plant evidently works, but it is gone for ever. Gilgamesh sits down, defeated, weeping, and says:

> Everything is lost now, Urshanabi!
> What comfort and what cost now, Urshanabi?
> Who have I laboured for with this arm?
> Who has my blood churned for? Oh what harm
> have I done instead of good: a beast
> has smacked its lips upon a human feast

that might have been. I have nothing left.
What shall I say to my city?

In a sense, this final defeat of Gilgamesh is the beginning of his regeneration. Rather like Lear on the heath, he has to have everything stripped away in order to see things clearly and not to hanker after impossible goals. He was now thinking of others. He had meant to keep the plant in order to give its rejuvenating virtues to the elderly folk in Uruk, not to hide it away for use when he himself was old. He was beginning to come to terms with the fact that death was not to be avoided, and that the only immortality open to him was not perhaps such a bad one – the recording of his deeds, the fixing of his quest in human memory – maybe not for ever, but clay tablets are remarkably hard and time-resistant, and in any case, as the poem claims at the outset, in its opening lines:

> [He] set all his labours on a tablet of stone…
> See the tablet-box of cedar,
> release its clasp of bronze!
> Lift the lid of its secret,
> pick up the tablet of lapis-lazuli and read out
> the travails of Gilgamesh, all that he went through.
>
> (from *The Epic of Gilgamesh*,
> trans. Andrew George, Penguin Classics, 1999)

So, if the exploits of Gilgamesh were carved on stone or lapis-lazuli, there would be an even better chance of his survival, in history, in literature. The author himself seems to share something of his hero's desire for immortality, and partly by luck and by chance that desire has so far been fulfilled.

The wiser, chastened Gilgamesh arrives safely back in Uruk with the ferryman, who seems now to be a firm friend, possibly about to replace, beyond the scope of the poem, the dead Enkidu, as far as this could be done. At the end of the poem Gilgamesh invites Urshanabi to go up onto the great wall of the city and walk around, marvelling at its workmanship, preparing to see this as his new home. Enkidu and Urshanabi both come into the city from outside, Enkidu from the green world of the forests, Urshanabi from the green world of the waters and seas. It is hard not to feel that some part of the author's quest, if not that of Gilgamesh, was to bring the urban world and the natural world together. The civilising of Enkidu was disastrous, tragic, for him, yet his statue stands in the square as a reminder of the green world for all the citizens to ponder. The watery world of Urshanabi, which is both destructive, as in the story of the Flood, and yet life-giving too – indeed necessary to life – has been brought into the city as another reminder of the powers of nature. The author of the poem is proud of his city culture, its literature and music, its mathematics and astronomy, its trading wealth, its irrigation and engineering skills. But as references to the sacred cedars of Lebanon show (a very long way from southern Iraq), or references to a great Flood which might well have actually happened and haunted the memory or half-memory of generations, the author was well aware that there are things 'out there' in the non-civilised world to which the recently invented art of writing could give a second life, within an urban setting of scribes and readers. This was a new quest which he took up with great vigour and often with very moving effect.

Edwin Morgan

THE PLAY OF GILGAMESH

In those days, in those far-off days, in those days, in those distant days,
in those years, in those far-off years,
in olden times, after what was needed had become manifest,
in olden times, after what was needed had been taken care of,
after bread had been swallowed in the sanctuaries of the land,
after the ovens of the land had been fixed up with bellows,
after heaven had been parted from earth,
after earth had been parted from heaven,
after the name of mankind had been established...

(Translated from the Sumerian by Andrew George, *The Epic of Gilgamesh*,
Penguin Classics, 1999)

Characters in Order of Appearance

HAMMAN, *a court official*
NEDU, *a trapper*
SHAMHAT, *a sacred harlot*
ENKIDU, *a 'wild man'*
JESTER
GILGAMESH, *King of Uruk*
NINSUN, *mother of Gilgamesh*
HUMBABA, *guardian of the Cedar Forest*
SHAMASH, *the sun-god*
ISHTAR, *high priestess of the love-cult*
MAJOR-DOMO
BARBER
ANU, *father of the gods*
DOCTOR
SCORPION-MAN
SCORPION-WOMAN
SIDURI, *a tavern-keeper*
URSHANABI, *a ferryman*
ZIUSURA, *a survivor of the Flood*
ZIUSURA'S WIFE

Harlots, Guards, Prisoners, Transvestites,
Citizens, Petitioners, Attendants, Counsellors,
Armourers, Priests, Guests, the Bull of Heaven

The scene is the Sumerian city of Uruk, in southern Iraq, 2750 BC

Act One
Scene One

A market square in the great city of Uruk on the Euphrates, in ancient Sumer (what is today southern Iraq), 2750 BC. Strong brick walls. A ziggurat temple. Motley crowd strolling about. Bright clothes. Stalls, merchants. Afternoon. A busy scene in what is clearly a wealthy city. Yet there is a sense of unease, something oppressive. Armed soldiers suddenly pounce on two young men and haul them away; despite the struggles and shouts, no one dares to intervene. Similarly, there is a quick scream as a girl is snatched away in another part of the square. These are, in modern terms, 'the disappeared'. A trapper from the countryside, NEDU, *makes his way through the crowd. He is carrying pelts for sale, and talking to* HAMMAN, *a court official.*

HAMMAN
How's business then? I've seen you with more skins.
To be blunt, some of these look bound for the bins.

NEDU
I know, Hamman, it's true, it's a lean time.
You'd almost think trapping was a crime.
Actually you don't know half of it.

HAMMAN
So tell me.

NEDU
          An open cage, an empty pit.
That's what I find when I'm prowling on my rounds.
They've been set free, jumped off in leaps and bounds
into the woods, hares, goats, foxes, deer –
lose my livelihood, I thought? No fear!
I lay in wait one night, at the full moon,
in sight of my traps, very still, and quite soon
a figure strode from the thicket, unlatched a cage,
brought out a gazelle, a little beauty, stroked it,
examined it closely, grinned, spoke to it
as it trotted off. Then he stood up, who knows
what to call him, wild man, green man, woodwose –
shaking his hair, hair down his back, hair
everywhere, god knows how strong, sniffed the air
like an animal, animals all about him –

3

I was certainly not going to rout them! –
fearsome creature but not ugly, an apparition
like something nature's, not a god's, decision
had made a man of. Amazing –

HAMMAN
                              I know.
I know who it is, Nedu. His legends grow.
Enkidu is his name. He lives with the beasts.
Roots, fruits, berries, water are his feasts.
He has no love for the walls of Uruk.

NEDU
Well, at this rate he'll make me a crook,
patching and repatching pelts while profits are down!

HAMMAN
We have our own problem in this town,
which gives me an idea. Gilgamesh the king –
I speak carefully to your understanding –
is a grand man, but no one feels secure.
Everyone knows he's like a god, oh sure,
athletic, young, with looks that sink all sexes,
a man of destiny – so what is it vexes
us, his subjects, why is there fear in the streets?

NEDU
I felt it today –

HAMMAN
                    His wars, his walls, his feats
are not enough for him, his arrogance
burns us up, struts, leads us a dance.
Young women snatched from their husbands, their mothers,
young men too; our sisters, our brothers.
He ramps and stamps like a bull, never sated.
What happens to them? They were only created
to be destroyed. He savours them, spits them out.
They disappear. They disappear. A shout
and a scuffle and they're gone.

NEDU
                              A plan.
You said you had a plan.

4

HAMMAN
 The king's but a man,
he must be made to feel that. We'll face him
with a rival –

NEDU
 Enkidu!

HAMMAN
 – not to replace him
but make him see he doesn't rule the universe.
How's that for a scenario?

NEDU
 Chapter and verse,
perfect. Foxes and hares revert to me.
Citizen Enkidu, we salute thee!
– But how? he's as shy as one of his gazelles.

HAMMAN
Without overstraining of the brain-cells,
Nedu, it's simple. A woman. I know one –

NEDU
– more than one, I fancy –

HAMMAN
 – and he's undone.
One of the sacred harlots, you must have seen her
at the temple, Shamhat. Stunning. Lean her
against a wall, and the brick smoulders. She'd
get a pharaoh's mummy hard. Enkid-
u doesn't stand a chance. I'll fix it.
The birdie doesn't know the shutter clicks it.

They walk off separately, NEDU *to chaffer his last furs,* HAMMAN *towards
the temple. Late afternoon, a darkening scene. People are preparing to go home.
A gong booms from the temple.*

Scene Two

In the temple. Night. Oil-lamps are burning, throwing strange shadows. Dressing-table with metal mirrors, make-up, etc. SHAMHAT *and her colleagues, the* SACRED HARLOTS *whose duties require them to take part in various erotic rituals, are sitting around on chairs or couches in their night clothes, chatting, laughing, combing their hair. Beds in the background, with images of winged deities above them, are being prepared by* EUNUCHS. SHAMHAT *is the focus of attention.*

1ST HARLOT
Shamhat, we are *green* with envy. We'll not sleep!

2ND HARLOT
We shall be counting hairy thighs, not sheep!

3RD HARLOT
How does she do it? The best jobs every time!

SHAMHAT
Sisters, I give good service. I don't mime.

1ST HARLOT
Neither do we! –

2ND HARLOT
— well sometimes –

3RD HARLOT
— if we're tired –

SHAMHAT
I have some Indian tricks to keep me fired.
I can prolong the agony until
we're synchronised, and take an equal fill
of one unsimulated whoosh and wham –

1ST HARLOT
Oh, not at bedtime please!

SHAMHAT
— and those who sham
should give up being servants of the temple.

Women of the streets are their example.

2ND HARLOT
Well well, we'll try to keep the juices flowing.
Meanwhile, round your green man grass is growing –

3RD HARLOT
Six feet of snoring hunk among the heather –

2ND HARLOT
They say he needs no clothes, in any weather –

1ST HARLOT
They also say he's never seen a woman –

SHAMHAT
They say, they say. I swear if he is human
I'll have his head. What, has he lived, the man?
(I call him man, he must be.) Will he ban
paradise if I show him it?

1ST HARLOT
                              Don't forget
he runs with panthers – the smell, the sweat –

SHAMHAT
There are springs. Perhaps he bathes as much as we do.
A little sweat won't keep me from Enkidu.

Temple gong sounds. She stretches, yawns.

Sisters, girls, it is late. I must be spry
tomorrow, and solemn too, with a smouldering eye
and a loose girdle, and all my senses drawn
to the breath and flutter of my skin; my finest lawn
will float from my shoulders; the circlet of the god
will glitter in my hair; I glide gold-shod
into the groves where I fulfil my duty,
and bring my husky bear back to the city.
Sisters, wish me well. The night is not long.
Let us please the gods of darkness with a song.

Music. During the singing of the song, the EUNUCHS *gradually extinguish
the lamps.*

Shadows of the evening, fold us.
Spirits of repose, hold us.
Let silence fall
where we lie down
at no one's beck and call,
and dream of nothing, nothing at all.

This one night, no man come near us,
no priests, no brutes, no interferers.
Virgin sheets,
pillows of down,
bless our brief retreats.
Tomorrow all is tricks and treats.

Our mothers smiled as they gave us away.
Great honour this, my girl, they'd say.
Your legs are wide
for king or clown
or god himself, you're the bride
of all, the bride who never cried,

the bride of all, who never cried.

Blackout. Exeunt.

Scene Three

Inside the state prison. Two GUARDS *are bringing in some new*
PRISONERS, *young men and women, struggling but chained together. Insults
are shouted from those already behind bars.* GUARDS *crack whips till things
calm down.*

1ST GUARD (*to new* PRISONERS)
Scum. Get in line! Fresh from the streets, eh?
Plotting and prowling, you think it's so easy
to slag the state or to finger the king.
It's not, you know, as you'll find out. A ring –
or two – of iron screwed in sensitive places

8

will re-set social thinking on a proper basis.
That basis is power. Don't kick against the pricks.
There's nothing wrong the common man can fix.
There's nothing wrong, period.

1ST PRISONER
                                I think there is.
I think the king should listen. The people are his –

2ND GUARD (*laughs*)
Of course the people are his! He does what he likes
with the people. He watches and he strikes.
Why should he even wait for discontent?
He pulls a few in, every week. It's meant
for terror, you know, terror?

2ND PRISONER
                        But why, why?

1ST GUARD
Who questions kings? You in a hurry to die?
He does what he does.

2ND PRISONER
                        Is he a god?

1ST GUARD
                            Who knows?
He's flesh and blood, as you'll soon see. He goes
from cell to cell, with a minder who's had his tongue
cut out. We would have ours cut out and hung
on the jail door like a fox's brush if we blabbed
a word of what goes on. I've seen guards stabbed
for raising eyebrows. The minder's quick as a snake.
So keep your dissident traps shut for chrissake

3RD PRISONER
I'm not a dissident!

1ST GUARD
                        You heard what I said.

2ND GUARD
He's coming. Stand straight, look straight ahead.

Enter GILGAMESH *and his* MINDER. *The king though not dressed royally (perhaps he has some sort of cloak) since he is engaged in clandestine activity, is a commanding figure. The* GUARDS *spring to attention and salute, shouting in unison 'Gilgamesh!'. That is the only word spoken in this part of the scene.* GILGAMESH, *with the* MINDER *at his side, moves slowly along the line of new prisoners, examining them as if at a slave auction. He feels their muscles, turns them round to scrutinise back as well as front, runs his hand over various parts of their bodies, looks fixedly at their faces. Occasionally he nods to the* MINDER, *who uses his stylus to write something on a clay tablet. All this is in silence, apart from the clanking of chains as a prisoner is moved about. The scene is all the more sinister because the king's purpose is never made clear — whether he dooms a prisoner to a particular punishment, adds him to a select band of Turkish-style janissaries, or singles out him or her for some sexual services. These various possibilities can be suggested by the king's actions. When he has finished examining the prisoners, he and his* MINDER *face the* GUARDS *and closely inspect them as they stand motionless and impassive. The king gives a nod, the* GUARDS *salute and shout 'Gilgamesh!' as before.* GILGAMESH *and the* MINDER *exeunt. Before they disappear, some hidden prisoner in the background shouts a half-comprehensible insult.* GILGAMESH *sweeps back, stands with hands on hips, and stares in the direction of the shout. There is silence, which holds as he eventually moves off stage.*

1ST GUARD
 Right, that's it. Nothing happened. No one
 saw anything. Scum to the cells. The sun
 will soon be up. Rolls and beer time. A crust
 may reach the cells. Later I might thrust
 a steak through the bars: he starves some, fattens some,
 did you know that? Don't ask me why. I'm dumb,
 as it's not dumb to be, I can assure you.
 Get in now, a little discipline will cure you.

1ST PRISONER
 The king is a bastard.

1ST GUARD
     I didn't hear that. Get in.
 The first thing you must learn is, you can't win.

Both GUARDS *laugh. Crack of whip. The* PRISONERS *are driven in.*

10

Scene Four

At the edge of a small wood, not far from Uruk. Bright sunshine. Suggestion of animals and birds moving among the undergrowth. Sounds of nature on a hot midday. The shaggy but impressive figure of the young 'wild man' ENKIDU emerges from the wood. He wears very little – perhaps a belt with a knife. He sings or chants his hymn to the sun-god, Shamash.

ENKIDU
Praise to the golden eye of Shamash as he bends to us from the blue.
He warms us from his far pavilions and sends us armfuls of light.
The seeds of this green place move and spring at his command.
The creatures of this green place multiply as he would wish.
He watches over the wild places and wild things with special affection.
Sometimes he is hard to us, makes deserts, but we trust him.
Ride the blue chariot, golden Shamash, till day is done!

The temple harlot, SHAMHAT, appears and walks slowly towards ENKIDU with practised (but not vulgar) seductiveness. She wears a simple robe with nothing underneath. Perhaps she has a fan or a whisk. She has a headdress to indicate her important (sacred) status as a priestess. Somehow it must be shown that she is not a common prostitute, is not involved in monetary transactions.

SHAMHAT
Enkidu, why so solemn, this fine day?

ENKIDU
If it is solemn, it is nature's way.

SHAMHAT
You think the sun won't shine unless you sing?

ENKIDU
I know the sun. He shines. He is my king.

SHAMHAT
There is another king in Uruk town.

ENKIDU
So I have heard. Out here, who needs a crown?

SHAMHAT
Out here? What sort of life? A wood, a field?

11

ENKIDU
Better a wee bush than nae bield.

SHAMHAT
That is too Babylonian for me.

ENKIDU
I don't climb thrones. I'm safer with a tree.

SHAMHAT
It's a poor life that never takes a risk.

ENKIDU
Our fate is written in the sun's disk.

SHAMHAT
My mistress, Ishtar, sees it in the moon.

ENKIDU
The moon's for women. Men give thanks at noon.

SHAMHAT
Are you a man? Can you do what a man does?

ENKIDU
I have fire, shelter. Hear my saw buzz!

SHAMHAT
That is not what I meant.
(*She moves closer to him and opens her robe*)
                                                    What do you see?

ENKIDU
Something I have never seen. Am I free
to touch the forest beasts but never this?

SHAMHAT
You are free as any man, to hold, to kiss.
Men say (and women too, I might just add)
I am well made, and though I have been had
as many times as ritual requires
in our great temple, I still keep desires
for such as you, and there's none such as you,
I think, Enkidu. Come with me, Enkidu.

Show me the grass and mosses where you lie.
Will they bear two of us? If you are shy –

ENKIDU
If I am, you must draw me on and on.
It is as if I had left oblivion
for the first time, I take steps in wonder.
Is it delusion I've been labouring under?
Forest power seems a hoax, a cheat,
as I watch sunlight shining on your cheek.
The sun, I thought I worshipped it! I do,
yet it seems pagan, alien, beside you.
Who are you to take me from my beasts?
You are the alien. After our love-feasts
the animals will never eat with me again.
They'll smell man, woman, cities, it's amen
to nature's bond. What can I do? – that skin,
that flesh, the way you move, it's in and in
until I am all crammed and glowing with it.
I am yours, in darkest bower, beyond my wit.

They go together into the wood.

Scene Five

The market square in Uruk, as in Scene 1. Citizens, merchants, good-time girls, soldiers, musicians. Preparations for a wedding. A young merchant and attractive bride are being slowly and elaborately robed up, with attendants, priestesses, etc. A festive scene, with conversation, laughter, and tentative bursts of music from musicians in background practising for the ceremony. Light taps on a drum become louder as the court JESTER, *who has the drum slung over his shoulder, weaves his way through the crowd, dancing, making gestures, perhaps goosing the more respectable citizenry, and addresses the audience.*

JESTER (*speaks in prose*)
See weddins? Waste a money. A thoosan widny cover this yin. Luk at
the lassie – Egyptian cotton, Indian silk, drippin wi gold an lapis-lazuli
– aye, an it is gold tae, nane a yer tin an a dip,– an him like a Persian
peacock, tryin tae dae a bit strut in aw that brocade – aye well, ye're
young wance Ah suppose, good luck tae them. Ah canny get merrit
masel, it widny dae for the king's jester. State secrets – an some a them

13

wid make yer hair curl – are safe wi me when Ah've gote nae Delilah
nor Mata Hari sharin ma pillow. Ah kin say whit Ah like – that's ma
joab – but Ah'm no daft. The last jester hud his face locked up in a
bress cage. No thanks. But Ah dae keep pushin at things when Ah smell
sumhm wrang. Aw, thae Stasi hitmen that prowl aboot the squerr –
whit're they up ti? Whit's the king up ti, that's mer tae the pynt. Aw
thae lads an lassies, aw thae *disappeared* wans, naebdy knows whit
happens ti them. Secret boadygaird? Target practice for his erchers?
Cock-practice for hissel? – everyone knows he's randy, but is he
polyfuckinmorphous-perverse tae? Okay a king's a king, an he gies
them bread an circuses ti stoap their moanin, but it's no right, it's no
right, an Ah telt'm as much. Oh christ, here's the circus! (*Beats drum
with mocking flourish*)

Enter festive chorus of TRANSVESTITES, *as part of wedding warm-up.
Music. Dance.*

TRANSVESTITES
    We love the gods, the gods love us.
    We're foolish but we're gorg-e-ous.
    Our eyes are black, our lips are red,
    and once you take us to your bed,
    is it bow-wow or is it miaow?
    Well it's wow!

    We like to flaunt our bit of flesh
    at festivals, for Gilgamesh.
    Pay us in dollars, dinars, kronor,
    we are the universal donor.
    How come such bosom and such basque? –
    never ask!

    We really are so *civilised*
    our eyebrows cannot be surprised.
    You want it here, you want it there,
    a toe, or a revolving chair –
    so who's the bride and who's astride?
    Oh you're wide!

    Our fishnets have the broadest mesh
    in honour of King Gilgamesh.
    We're not the servants of the state.
    We're just ourselves, and that's our fate.
    We're just ourselves, my dears, hey hey,
    we're away!

A stir among the crowd. ENKIDU *enters, led by* SHAMHAT, *who has made him put on some clothes (but not enough to conceal his size and strength). The wild man has never been seen in the city before. She leads him to a table, offers him drink. He gulps quickly – his first taste of alcohol. Soon people drift towards the table.*

VOICES IN CROWD
> Enkidu! – It's Enkidu! – Look at the size of
> him! – Not as big as Gilgamesh! – Younger though! –
> Those arms! – All that hair! (*etc.*)

HAMMAN *and* NEDU *are seen in the crowd, exchanging glances and signs of pleasure that their plan has so far succeeded.*

SHAMHAT
> Seven nights of love! You must build up
> your strength, Enkidu. Sit down, eat, sup.
> I tempt you with some tender venison –

ENKIDU (*exclaims and recoils with disgust*)
> A deer's my family! How could I eat my son!

SHAMHAT
> I have made you a man. You must eat man's food.
> Try it. Try it. A little. Is it not good?
> Sumerian cooks are surely no mean sutlers.
> Our brilliant bottles please the prickliest butlers.
> – You see? You like it? Wash it down with beer.
> The tankard, the tankard, not the bowl, my dear!

ENKIDU *is beginning to enjoy himself. The drink makes him loquacious.*

ENKIDU
> I tell you – Shamhat – friends – Uruk citizens –
> The forest is a wonderful place, and its denizens –
> now there's a word I like, they live in dens
> the ones I love – are no longer mine, or men's,
> but only nature's. I, she, we broke the link.
> I've eaten flesh, and water's not my drink.
> But I must say this drink is very very –
> I do feel different – it's extraordinary –
> the woods, the lions, doves, gazelles are fading
> no more panting, pawing, purring, parading –
> scents of Shamhat have killed the fetid pelts

I used to mingle sweat with – buckles and belts
are good to feel instead of ivies and snakes –
I never thought I'd think so – see these cakes,
these cakes, I don't know who made them, but
they're absolutely – picture me gnawing a nut
a week ago under a walnut tree
and calling it a banquet – now I'm free,
I'm free, my friends, the green world and the red
meet in my veins and here you see a head
that swings all round Uruk and smells misgivings.
I have come to change the nature of things.
(*He bangs tankard on table*)
Where's Gilgamesh?

SHAMHAT
                    Be patient, he'll soon be here.
Be wary too, he's a man of moods. Fear
follows his stride. Anxiety stares out
from doorways. A murmur, not a shout
acknowledges his progress. Something black
sits in his soul. Yet Uruk has no lack:
our wealth, our walls, our temples – where's their match?
Nowhere in this middle world! Like a great catch
from the Euphrates we dance in silver, soon to die.
He reigns, he builds, his brick soars to the sky.
He is like a god; perhaps he is a god.
Can you tangle with gods, Enkidu?

ENKIDU
                    God, schmod.

SHAMHAT
Don't drink so much. You are not used to it.

ENKIDU
Never felt better, darlin'. Fighting fit.

*A gong announces the end of the marriage ceremony, which has been continuing
in the background. A priest joins the hands of the bride and groom, who walk
slowly forward, surrounded by friends and wellwishers throwing flowers. Harps
are played. The table where* SHAMHAT *and* ENKIDU *are sitting becomes
part of a general celebration. But suddenly soldiers crack whips and open up the
crowd for the entrance of* GILGAMESH. *Harsh but impressive fanfare of
trumpets and drums.* GILGAMESH *enters with retinue, sweeps his eyes
through the crowd, and walks swiftly towards the wedding couple.*

GILGAMESH

> Established custom, strong, unalterable,
> divides the married from the marriageable,
> but none is truly married till the king
> has stepped between the husband and his ring.
> The first fruits of this lady, who I see
> sways like a palm of price, must fall to me.
> Leave his hand; my bed waits; (*to attendant*) take her.

ENKIDU springs forward and places himself in front of the bride.

ENKIDU

> No! She will not go. Nothing will make her.
> She is her husband's woman, his is her bed.

GILGAMESH

> What lout is this? Carry on and you're dead.

ENKIDU

> I am no lout, but a free man whom you know,
> Enkidu, come from the wilderness to show
> how soon I mean to change the order of things.

GILGAMESH (*laughs*)
First then you have to take the measure of kings.

*They strip for a wrestling-match. The crowd, whispering and muttering
excitedly, falls back to give them space. They wrestle, a gigantic and protracted
struggle, breaking tables and doorposts etc. in the process. They are fairly
evenly matched except that ENKIDU should not have drunk so much and may
have been weakened by his seven days and nights of love with SHAMHAT.*

VOICE FROM THE CROWD

> A throw!

ANOTHER VOICE

> No no, he's up!

A THIRD VOICE

> Come on Enkidu!

*Soldiers move menacingly among the crowd, as ENKIDU seems to be winning.
But the strength and experience of GILGAMESH begin to tell.*

17

1ST VOICE
Look at that!

2ND VOICE
Is he down?

3RD VOICE
No – slipped through.

GILGAMESH *using his leg as a lever overthrows* ENKIDU *and immediately pins him flat, straddles him, and claims victory. Mixed reaction from crowd: some groan, some shout, some clap. A pause. Then the two men stand up and embrace. Burst of clapping from crowd.*

ENKIDU
Gilgamesh, you have great strength, and fight fair.
I believe no one is like you anywhere.
The gods gave you all power: use it well.

GILGAMESH
Enkidu, what gods give no man can tell.
They give, they take away. But I say here
I have found a brother devoid of fear
who challenged the ruler of the world (for so
men call me) and stood the course. Do not go
back to the grim forest. My palace is yours.
We shall do something. These are our overtures.

ENKIDU
And the bride?

GILGAMESH
She is free. And give her this.
(*Takes off a ring and hands it to an attendant*)
Brother, let us go in. You will not miss
the wilderness, I promise you. Give us some robes.
Have you seen torches set in porcelain globes?

Exeunt with retinue. It is evening. The crowd gradually disperses, buzzing.

JESTER
Aye well, all buddies noo. Whit can come o that, eh? Whit kinna cratur is thon hairy wan? He's no canny if ye ask me. Brought up wae monkeys an plowterin through cowpats? Kin the monkey chynge his

18

spoats? The temple lassie has gien him boxers an a shirt an a whiff o auld spice, but *brithers*? Kin the king an the wolf-boay be brithers? Ah'm no a class activist but there is limits. Never mind. (*Gives his drum a bang or two*) It's a great place is Uruk if ye dinny weaken. See thae high waws – best brick in the business – brilliant – naebdy kin invade us. 'Course ye need a pass tae get oot – but that's life. Religious processions, street theaytre, barbecues – nut a dull moment. Dungeons let oot tae private tender – they say it's like a hame fae hame doon therr, which Ah canny credit, kin you? (*Sings*)

> The lord, the lord, the lord Gilgamesh'll
> take ye aside an gie ye sumhm special.

Ah didny say that. Ah only sung it. A sang's no an affidavit, Fundamentally he's no such a bad lad, if only (Ah'd better sing that tae):

> If only sumbdy could knoak some sense intae him
> an take him doon a peg or two – no slay him.

Mibbe thon Tarzan is jist the ticket efter aw. But Ah'll keep an eye on the baith o them, that's for sure. (*Bangs on drum*)

Scene Six

A room in the palace. Two chairs. It is the morning after the wrestling-match. Gilgamesh's mother, NINSUN, *is sitting on one of the chairs, sewing.* GILGAMESH *is prowling up and down.*

GILGAMESH
  Dreams, mother, nightmares! What am I to think?

NINSUN
  Last night you had too much to eat and drink.

GILGAMESH
  I'm serious. I woke sweating, twice. Two dreams.

NINSUN
  I have to watch the new line of these seams.

GILGAMESH
    Mother!

NINSUN
            I'm listening. Some of us can do
    two things at once, you know. So tell me true.
    And use that chair for goodness sake.

GILGAMESH *sits.*

GILGAMESH
        All right!
    But something was being said to me last night.
    I dreamed I was out walking with some friends,
    one of these fine evenings heaven sends
    to soothe our cooling fields. The soft black sky
    was starry, starry – would make astronomers cry
    to see so clear and near a zodiac –
    there was one with us, almost on his back
    craning to trace a favourite constellation –
    when suddenly we jumped – consternation –
    a flash, a hiss, a quickly falling mass
    of meteorite flattened and singed the grass.
    Dark, big, come from nowhere, from space,
    it challenged me to lift it. With a grimace
    I strained and tried, strained and failed. I swore,
    we all came crowding round, then more and more
    people appeared, came from the city, knelt there
    as if it was a black slab flown from Jupiter,
    kissed it, the rock, the thing, I kissed it too,
    embraced it, sweating and swearing, shot through
    with – mother, I tell you I was in love with it!
    This is mad –

NINSUN (*laying down her sewing and looking hard at her son*)
            Nothing is beyond our wit
    to interpret –

GILGAMESH
            Mother, I loved it like a wife,
    lifted it at last, laid it at your feet. The strife,
    you said, the sweat, you said, were good.
    You said it must compete with me. I stood
    with my hands spread, baffled. Then I woke –

20

NINSUN

    Shooting-stars, comets, meteorites – at a stroke
    they usher change, remind us that the universe,
    though constant-seeming, has no chapter and verse
    engraved in everlasting cuneiform.
    Shamash rises, but days are not uniform.
    One *coup de foudre* – I like that Egyptian phrase –
    can shatter even the most settled ways.
    Gilgamesh, the meteorite is that man
    who has dropped into your orbit by some plan
    of gods among the stars, if such there are,
    that man of woods and wilds, that deodar
    whose branches must be intertwined with yours.
    You wrestled with a thunderbolt. The cures
    for wilfulness are unforeseen but great.
    How could you know you wrestled with your fate?
    Enkidu is your friend and will protect you.
    Love him, and let nothing human deflect you.

GILGAMESH

    But I'm the king. I can't divide my rule!

NINSUN

    Why not? Think about it. Put your pride to school.

GILGAMESH

    Pride? I am a king, and you are the mother
    of a king. If we can't be proud, can any other?

NINSUN

    My son, you have so many things to learn
    you frighten me. Are you never to earn
    more than your people's fear? Kowtow-time? Power?

GILGAMESH *looks sulky.* NINSUN *takes up her sewing again.*

    Tell me your other dream.

GILGAMESH

                Some daylight hour
    this time, the sun was up, the streets were loud.
    Just at the palace gate, there was a crowd
    collecting, one or two at first, then many,
    eyes on the ground as if a diamond penny

had landed there, and certainly there was a flash,
but something more impressive than dropped cash.
I almost stumbled over it: a huge axe.
The helve was broad, curved, carved with snaky tracks
for a good hold, the blade would have cut trees –
heads – doorposts – bronze shields – jailers' iron keys –
it shone, winked, shone, as if a light inside
was signalling, 'Lift me, I am your bride.'
I bent down, clasped it, hugged it to me, brought
the weight of it, the flash of it, without a thought,
driven, mesmerised, back to you. You said
it must compete with me. An axe-head?!
An axe from nowhere, alien, non-Sumerian?

NINSUN
Sumer will not be saved by Sumer. The serum
must be found elsewhere. If something is amiss –
and I know something is amiss, and the kiss
you gave the axe and meteorite reveals
your dreaming reason only half conceals
that *you* know something is amiss – it's time
to teach the stranger vine to twist and climb.
You never saw the likes of your dream-axe,
but that is good, not bad. It will never be lax
in your defence, but it will not defend you
against yourself. Love it, it will bend you
out of the ramrod fevers that would break you.
The blade, Enkidu, has cut through to wake you.

Enter ENKIDU, *slightly dishevelled and hungover, but still rather*
magnificent. It is now nearly midday, and the room has been gradually growing
lighter during the previous scene. Suddenly it becomes very bright, and the room
itself recedes into shadow. GILGAMESH, NINSUN *and* ENKIDU *stand*
together (in that order) facing the audience, in a strong light, and speak (or
sing) ritualistically, like principals in an opera. Music – a strange mixture of
the lyrical and the ominous.

GILGAMESH
I thought my thoughts were solid
but they're melting into air.
I thought my dreams were rubbish
but they seem both real and rare.

NINSUN

    I see a king and his brother.
    I see them laugh, walk, talk.
    I see them sit, take counsel,
    and neither wears the frock.

ENKIDU

    I stretched in my four-poster.
    The woods were never like this.
    They brought me wine and water.
    I drank, washed, drank. What bliss.

GILGAMESH

    I threw him in the fighting.
    Is there an overthrow?
    In my dream the shining axe-head
    made me shiver first, then glow.

NINSUN

    When jailers roll their banknotes
    the king must turn the key.
    How will he learn his lesson
    at the tree of liberty?

ENKIDU

    He threw me in the fighting.
    Is there an overthrow?
    He has planted me beside him.
    Water me, and I grow.

GILGAMESH

    May I gain a friend and adviser,
    friend and adviser may I gain!
    May he drive out all my nightmares
    like dust across the plain!

NINSUN

    May they wrestle only at tables,
    with chessmen, not with men.
    If they have to hunt the lion,
    may they come home again.

ENKIDU

    May I please him, I have no one.

I had lions once, not now.
I must learn to love the city,
throne, chariot, dhow.

NINSUN
May they wrestle only at tables –

ENKIDU
May I please him, I have no one –

GILGAMESH
May he drive out all my nightmares –

The music continues, as they freeze in different gestures appropriate to their speeches. Blackout.

END OF ACT ONE

Act Two
Scene One

A few months later. An audience room in the palace. Twin thrones, on which GILGAMESH *and* ENKIDU *are seated, formally dressed. An attendant brings in a woman* PETITIONER *who kneels and bows before the thrones. The* TREASURER *stands beside the thrones with a bag of coins.*

GILGAMESH (*to attendant*)
I hope this is the last? (*Attendant nods and bows*)
                               Whole morning gone.
   wheedling appeals, petitions, on and on –

ENKIDU
   Keep that for later. You shame her. Let her plead –

GILGAMESH
   All right, all right. – Madam, do you bleed?

PETITIONER
   My lord – ?

GILGAMESH
                       Are you bereft, in penury,
   abandoned, a single parent, is usury
   biting your purse, has your number come up
   but you've lost your lottery ticket, oh it's some cup
   that runneth over, spill it before the king,
   the king is here to deal with everything –

ENKIDU
   Gilgamesh, for godsake –

GILGAMESH
                               – deal with the lot.
   Anyhow, anyhow. (*To the woman* PETITIONER) What have you not got
   that you want to have? (*To the* TREASURER) Your stylus? In writing.

PETITIONER
   Sir, my husband died in the last fighting
   down by the Gulf, in the marshes. I'm alone
   with two young children. I have never known

25

the fear a penny on the price of bread
can bring till now –

GILGAMESH
          This man of yours that's dead,
was he a regular in the royal army,
or was he some poor raggle-taggle mercenary?

PETITIONER
Sir, he was a corporal. His body was never found.

GILGAMESH
A corporal without a corpse? You're bound
to find that in the very worst taste, I know.
My tongue runs on, the lord Enkidu says so.
We'll not go into that. (*To the* TREASURER) Give her fifty.

ENKIDU
A hundred. There is no glory in being thrifty.

GILGAMESH *shrugs, nods agreement, dismisses* PETITIONER, *who rises, makes the slightest of bows, and exits with the* TREASURER. *He pockets the clay tablet he has been writing on. Coins chink in the bag as he bows to the thrones and exits.*

GILGAMESH *and* ENKIDU *prepare to relax after the morning's business, loosening their robes, taking off the royal headgear. As the light dims on the throne area, light comes up on a group of* ATTENDANTS *bringing in some refreshments. They set down a table and a couch, put a fine cloth on the table, and lay the table with jugs of wine, goblets, plates of cakes and sweetmeats, bowls of fruit and nuts, and a small jewelled box. They sing the*

SONG OF THE LITTLE REFRESHMENT

Once you've done a bit of business
you are ready for some vino.
Let your belt out, take a napkin,
oloroso or a fino,
oloroso or a fino.

Ice is tinkling in the tumbler,
all the peanuts are dry-roasted,
take a pastry, let it crumble,
best the bakers ever boasted,
best the bakers ever boasted.

26

Press a peach against your palate,
grip a grape and lift your elbow.
Crack a walnut, tell a story.
Cares of state fly out the window,
cares of state fly out the window.

Slurp a little, sniff a little.
Far off are the cries of battle.
Drop on your divans, my darlings.
Soon enough will branches rattle,
all too soon will branches rattle.

Exeunt ATTENDANTS. GILGAMESH *and* ENKIDU *stand up, leave the thrones and come down to the well-lit table area. They sit on the couch, where they are symbolically closer than on their separate thrones. Although the hoped-for plan to have* ENKIDU *undermine the arrogance of* GILGAMESH *has still some way to go, as could be observed from the scene with the* PETITIONER, *it is clear that the two men are already close friends who despite their arguments enjoy each other's company.* GILGAMESH *lifts the jewelled box from the table, takes a pinch of the white powder it contains, and snorts it. He passes the box to* ENKIDU *who does the same, though with less practised ease, as a country boy still feeling his way into the city's pleasures.* GILGAMESH *laughs.*

GILGAMESH
Go on, a little snort won't kill you!

ENKIDU (*shaking his head from side to side*)
                                        Ah!
They talk about the perfumes of Arabia
but this is – Ah! – much better –

GILGAMESH
                              It's the best.
So pure and fine we export it east and west.
Temples use it in their mysteries.
A little coke unlocks the ecstasies.
You don't have to believe me. Try a peach –
it's the aftertaste – you're stretched out on the beach
at midnight, stars are shooting down on you
till you tingle like Sebastian – Enkidu!
Enkidu! – you hear them? Mind the stone.

ENKIDU
A good thing we don't do this on the throne.

GILGAMESH
Oh I don't know. We might be kinder souls.
Pour me some of the red.

ENKIDU
                              What are our goals?
To make the people less afraid of us –

A drumbeat is heard offstage. Then the JESTER *strides into view, wearing a mock crown.*

JESTER
Who's afraid then? Who's feart, eh? No me. How's it gaun,
Gilgamaister? Okay Enkidu-boay? (*He perches on the couch, and sings*)

    Three kings sat upon the waw
    Sat upon the waw
    Sat upon the waw
    Three kings sat upon the waw
    On a cauld and frosty mornin.

(*He jumps down from the couch*) The question is, sirs, sirrahs, maisters,
the great and pressin question is – an Ah fin masel in a kinna
philosophomoric frame a mind, the day – the hithertoheretofore-
unformulatit crux or crutch a the maitter is, Can even *twa* kings sit
upon the waw?

ENKIDU *throws him some fruit, which he catches.*

Thank ye kindly, but ye'll no pit me aff ma dissertation wi bribes and
prezzies. Accordin tae the sages of the last millennium, when Sumer
wiz hoatchin wi shamans and wizards and wysiwygs, ye canny get two
tae go intae wan. Take two kings. We'll no take three, that's ower
complicated (*throws off his mock crown*). Wan king says, 'Bring uz the
heid of Alfredo Garcia.' The ither king says, 'Naw, bring uz his scalp,
let his faimly keep the heid.' Ye canny go oan like that. Oh aye. Ah
know whit ye're goany say, you twos are different, youse are sworn
brithers, youse are twin harmonies, you set yir watches thegither an
that's Sumerian time.

GILGAMESH *and* ENKIDU, *indulgently playing along with the* JESTER, *smile at each other and mime the setting of their watches.*

It's no a joke, no really. Jist look at ye, lyin therr like couch potatoes.
Aye aye, enjoy yir pairty, enjoy yir wee honeymoon. But whit aboot the
kingdom, whit aboot the people, whit aboot the universe? Ye think thae
big strang waws'll keep the universe oot? No if ye're slurpin an
smoochin – sorry, that's no the word, that jist slipped oot – moochin,
slurpin an moochin aw the day. Ye've gote tae shake yirsels (*bangs
drum*), get oot therr an dae sumhm (*bangs drum*), get thae muscles toned
up till they're like loupin saumon (*bangs drum with a flourish*)! C'moan,
Big Gilgamac, ye're the king a no mean city, let's see some action, an
Ah dinny mean hucklin the lieges. Keep at him, Enkidu boay, you're
supposed tae *help* him. D'ye hink, because ye've gote cakes an ale,
there's tae be nae merr virtue? And eftir these weel-siftit words

> Ah'll jist pick up ma wee bit croon,
> see if Ah kin sell it doon the toon.

(*He picks up the mock crown, and dances off to irregular drum-beats.*
GILGAMESH *rises and stretches, wiping mouth, brushing crumbs,*
straightening robes.

GILGAMESH
He's right, you know. We've had three months of – what?
Eating, drinking, the court, the accounts, a spot
of mild safari, inspecting the palace guard,
signing execution slips – well that's not hard,
that's not a life, that won't get me carved
in eternal characters, I feel half-starved
of greatness. Sure, I built the city wall;
Uruk is great, a beacon, a refuge; all
Mesopotamia knows me, it, you. Who'd
attack us? Pharaohs? Nah. I've stood
beside our ziggurats that step to heaven
in lapis-lazuli and gold, shining in the oven
of Shamash, juggernauts to storm the gods,
tempt a divine task force? What's the odds?
No divine task force. Maybe nothing up there.
We're so secure, what is there to do for a dare
unless we give ourselves that dare? We could –

ENKIDU
What?

GILGAMESH

      – renew the Great Gate if we had some wood.

ENKIDU

  I came from woods –

GILGAMESH

             – but our timber's not strong.
  I think we have a journey, very far, very long.
  North-west, to Mount Lebanon, into the snow,
  up to those ridges where the cedars grow.
  We'll fell the trees, make rafts of them, and float
  our gate down the Euphrates boat by boat.

ENKIDU (*uneasy, as a lover of forests, a 'green man'*)
  Oh Gilgamesh, you have forgotten one thing:
  someone there will never let you bring
  his wood back to Uruk. His are the cedars,
  he guards them with his life, as all the readers
  of our most ancient tablets know: his name
  is strange and his description stranger, his fame
  is terror: Humbaba, as the tablets record,
  roars like a flood, his mouth is fire, the word
  that issues with his breath is death. He hears
  a rustling from three hundred miles. He fears
  nothing except a bare Mount Lebanon.
  He is a kind of man, a dragon-man, a guardian.
  The forest is his. The gods have assigned it!

GILGAMESH

  The gods? Are there gods? Well, we shall find it,
  this forest. Ogres are for fairy-tales.
  Real-life ogres, yetis on the trails –
  Enkidu, we're not weaklings, yearlings, kids –
  we'll take them as they come. We make our bids
  for fame because we have to. Sure you love trees,
  but now you've left the brambles and the bees,
  you're not a wild man any more –

ENKIDU

                   I am –

GILGAMESH

  You're not. You're living in a capital town,

you're rolling Caspian caviar on your tongue,
and see your sheer silk shirts –

ENKIDU
                              – such sheer
silk shirts?

Both laugh.

GILGAMESH
             Know what I mean? It's clear
you are not purely green.

ENKIDU
                    I don't know –

GILGAMESH
Look, we'll ask the Counsellors to go
and cast their runes. On their positive say-so
will you be satisfied?

ENKIDU
                    I suppose so –

GILGAMESH (*puts arm round* ENKIDU*'s shoulder and gives it a squeeze*)
We'll go. kill right? We'll go. And we'll be armed.
The blacksmith's power will bring us back unharmed.

*Exeunt. The poem says 'hand in hand', as young men still do in Middle Eastern
countries, without any necessarily erotic implication. If the director senses a
problem with modern audiences, perhaps they could go arm in arm, or perhaps
some macho form of hand or wrist contact could be devised. The problem is that
there really* is *an unspoken erotic charge between the two men, which was first
felt in the wrestling scene and which will become more overt at a later stage in
the play.*

Scene Two

A small bare dark council-chamber. Strong light on a hard table and three chairs. Three middle-aged or elderly COUNSELLORS *are seated at the table. A scribe is taking notes with a reed pen on clay tablets.*

1ST COUNSELLOR
  Gentlemen, you know what Lord Gilgamesh has proposed.
  Our Great Gates are warped, imperfectly closed.
  The king is set on a timber expedition
  to the cedars of Lebanon. The position
  is clear: he rules, he orders life, he goes
  if he wants to go. But he also knows
  (when he remembers it) that our advice
  is serious, and even if it cuts no ice
  with him, it is recorded. So: your views.

2ND COUNSELLOR
  I am not happy. I think it is bad news.
  The forests of Lebanon are guarded by a creature
  some say is more than mortal; every feature
  described by no doubt exaggerated report
  is terrible: a roar to shake our fort,
  a furnace mouth, a toxic breath, senses
  more animal than human. What defences –
  the king is but a man after all – exist
  to bring him back to us, best and greatest
  for all his faults we're like to see? Enkidu
  would go with him, but what can even he do?
  Are there any men of strength that would not run
  when the earth quakes with a thundering ton
  of Humbaba proving his sacred vigilance?
  Too risky: that is my deliverance.

3RD COUNSELLOR
  Our lord the king is in the prime of life,
  needs scope, needs testing, danger, challenge, strife.
  He's a loose cannon here, with nothing to do.
  Let him see this wild adventure through.
  I watched him pull a lion's head right back
  once, on safari, till I heard it crack.
  Humbaba is not dealing with a nerd.

Do we think glory is only to be inferred,
imputed? Let Gilgamesh be kitted out
as warrior king. Stand by him. He has my shout.

1ST COUNSELLOR
Gentlemen, I have the casting vote.
Hunger for fame is like an asymptote
stretching for ever into the unknown,
far from the padded purple of a throne.
Gilgamesh has that hunger, will never lose it.
He is learning – slowly – how not to abuse it.
On the white ridge of Lebanon he will meet
terrors to brace or break him. If his feat
succeeds, his restless spirit may be sated
at least until some new desire's created.
We must persuade Enkidu to be his guide,
his scout, his avant-garde, either at his side
or in front, he knows forests, let him be
responsible, he loves him, he is the key.
We counsel then: a high noon for Humbaba.
Give the forge the gist of our indaba.

Exeunt.

Scene Three

*The royal forge. Clash of metal, beating of hammers, hiss of blades in water. A
furnace, an anvil, bellows, tongs, flame and smoke.* ARMOURERS *at work,
including a woman. Bantering conversation, snatches of song.*

1ST ARMOURER
Christ, there's a hole in the bellows!

2ND ARMOURER
                              Take the spare,
somewhere yonder.

3RD ARMOURER
                  What d'you bet it's not there?

33

1ST ARMOURER

I've got it. Time this fire was really *blown*.
These rush jobs —

2ND ARMOURER

          — best you've ever known —
double time, tub of beer —

3RD ARMOURER

              — but why the hurry?

The WOMAN ARMOURER *steps forward.*

SONG OF THE LESBIAN BLACKSMITH

Skelp the sparks and watch them scurry,
sniff the smoke-clouds as they flurry,
squat down on the dirty durrie.
Leather and iron, iron and leather,
our cavern is dark whatever the weather,
but we have a dark and glorious job to do,
bright weapons for Gilgamesh and Enkidu.

Get them well armed, sworded, daggered,
as they stride to strike the blackguard,
leave him stunned and slashed and staggered.
Blizzard and forest, forest and blizzard,
watch out for the wily wizard,
hack his head and take those trees and be true
to your dreams, great Gilgamesh and Enkidu.

Best of bronze blades for the brawny,
burnish them all brisk and bonny,
gild the scabbards rich and tawny.
Helm and hip, hip and helm
may no demons overwhelm,
and let this sooty forge keep death from you,
my brothers Gilgamesh and Enkidu.

1ST ARMOURER

Last check, and we're ready. Broadswords?

2ND ARMOURER

              Two.

1ST ARMOURER
 Daggers?

3RD ARMOURER
 Two.

1ST ARMOURER
 Axes?

2ND ARMOURER
 There *were* two. Who – ?

1ST ARMOURER
 Guys, this is not a party. Where the hell –

3RD ARMOURER
 It's here, it's here.

1ST ARMOURER
 Thank christ for that. Well,
there should be two helmets and two shields –

2ND ARMOURER
 Right.

3RD ARMOURER
 Right.

1ST ARMOURER
 And when they get to the high fields,
the snowy places, two jerkins, leather, tough –

2ND ARMOURER
 Big. These are for big men.

1ST ARMOURER
 It's quite enough
to tell me they're *there*, never mind the *size*.

3RD ARMOURER
 Here they are. Dead weight too.

1ST ARMOURER
 You realise

everything's been measured to the last millimetre,
the last ounce. Even a panel-beater
could see the quality. We're pros, they're heroes.

3RD ARMOURER
They're pros, *we're* heroes. No, I'm quite serious.
Isn't it heroic to swap a poor pay-packet
for sweat, burns, cuts, all this unholy racket?

2ND ARMOURER
At least we're not slaves, captives, forced enlisters.
Buy some ear-plugs. Bandage up your blisters.

A distant trumpet sounds. They listen.

1ST ARMOURER
Bandage up your mouths. That's the announcing
of the expedition. Great. Fucking trouncing
of Humbaba. Everything packed, stacked?
Gilgamesh has got that ogre whacked.

2ND ARMOURER
And Enkidu.

3RD ARMOURER
              Plus us.

1ST ARMOURER
              Okay, spread the glory.
Poets will come to hammer out this story.

The LESBIAN BLACKSMITH *is spotlighted as she stands up with a large hammer and strikes a ringing blow on the anvil. Blackout.*

Scene Four

The journey of GILGAMESH *and* ENKIDU *north-west to Mount Lebanon takes them several months, with overnight stops to set up camp, and with the weather gradually changing from the heat of Uruk to the cold of the Lebanese mountains. Music and sound-effects, plus miming of the trek, but no dialogue. A revolving stage would be good; or perhaps strobe lighting. The two men set off, with their weapons and backpacks, to farewell cheers from the (unseen) citizens of Uruk; springy step, sunshine, upbeat music. As time passes, the journey becomes more difficult, the music less upbeat. Sometimes* GILGAMESH *is in the lead, sometime* ENKIDU. *Sometimes they temporarily lose the way, stop, argue. Once, their nerves fray, and they fight, but soon realise this is futile, and go forward together. It is now much colder, and the two men pause and put on their leather jerkins, and have to struggle upwards against the wind, and eventually light flurries of snow. The music and the wind merge into the sense of a harsh, alien, yet beautiful world: the high ridge of Mount Lebanon. There is now a visible scene: snow-capped mountains, rocky paths with patches of snow and the thick forest of magnificent cedars.* GILGAMESH *and* ENKIDU *take off their packs, stand, look, and listen.*

GILGAMESH
The trees, the trees, Enkidu, the trees at last!

ENKIDU
Oh it's worth all the dangers we have passed!

GILGAMESH
How pure the air is! Can this be a haunted place?

ENKIDU
Nature has powers when we're face to face.

GILGAMESH
The waterfalls, the chack of choughs, the wind!

ENKIDU
I feel light-headed, the atmosphere's so thinned.

GILGAMESH
Dangerous to rest. We must be up and doing.

ENKIDU
Dangerous to start our own undoing.

GILGAMESH
What? You have second thoughts, at this stage?

ENKIDU
I always had, as you well know. We wage –

GILGAMESH
- war against principalities and powers?

ENKIDU
No, against taking what's not truly ours.

GILGAMESH
We've been through this before. You came with me.

ENKIDU
But now I see the bloody living tree!

GILGAMESH
It isn't about to live much longer. The axes!

ENKIDU
All right. I've only instinct, you've got praxis.

GILGAMESH
Don't pity yourself. You came. Now let's get going.

ENKIDU
Yes, we'd better start. It'll soon be snowing.

They take out their axes and begin chopping down the cedars. The sound carries through the still air, with the expected result. There is a loud roaring voice, followed by a crackling and crashing movement through the forest. HUMBABA, the guardian of the cedars, wearing a fearsome mask, emerges angrily into the clearing where the two axemen are mutilating what he has a mission to protect. He has a human shape and uses human speech, but he has claws for hands, and has some sort of body armour that makes him look slightly reptilian. He has a long red forked tongue which flicks in and out (this is what has given rise to the legends of his 'furnace mouth'). He should be genuinely frightening, and not grotesque or a pantomime figure of fun. Between him and ENKIDU there is a certain rapport, since both are 'green men', but HUMBABA hates and despises ENKIDU as a citified renegade from the world of nature. ENKIDU, caught between his recognition of HUMBABA as one of nature's guardians and his by now strong loyalty to GILGAMESH and Uruk, addresses HUMBABA ahead of GILGAMESH.

ENKIDU
Humbaba, we know you, and we know you guard
the cedar forest, which you think is barred
to all for ever, but it is not so.

You are cut off from the world, and cannot know
the greatest of its cities, and what it needs.
Our long haul here, our mission and our deeds
are authorised. Uruk's majestic gate
shakes on its hinges. We need timber. Fate
brings us to this place.

HUMBABA (*gives a horrible laugh*)
                  Fate? Authorised?
Are you not men, can't you be self-advised?
I know you both, I have my ear to the ground.
You, Gilgamesh, think glory's easily found.
You, Enkidu, are a running dog, a lackey.
Your opening speech, if I may call it that, is tacky.
Take yourselves back to metroland.

GILGAMESH (*laughs*)
                      Humbaba,
you think you are the absolute rum baba
but you've gone off, you're past your date. Is that coarse?
Kings are allowed to be coarse as a matter of course.
The wedge has not been made that you could drive
between Enkidu and me. To remain alive,
try something else.

HUMBABA
               No, I shall keep at it.
Two are not one, that's hardly mathematic.
I'd rather have a coarse king than a king
who trammels his coat-tails with a nobody, a nothing.
Enkidu, you son of a fish, do you know your father?
You haven't got one, or a mother, would you rather
we took our finger out and called you a bastard?
I hear your first act in the city was to get plastered.
Were you trying to win a bright red face, like Shamash?
Shamash should burn you up, you turd, you moron,
you kitchen-boy, you sook, you empty sporran.
You hang round Gilgamesh to gulp the crumbs
of kingship, but he has more *nous* in his thumbs
than you could strain your stringy brain to imagine,
your spirits like your boots too ropy to do a hajj in.

GILGAMESH (*holds back* ENKIDU *who is about to strike* HUMBABA)
Humbaba, you are wasting breath. We two

have come in our joint strength, not to undo
your green imperium but to remove
from its vast acres some few trees, and prove
the world is everyone's. Enkidu and I
will take what we want, and if you should try
to oppose us, we might take more than that,
and we might take you too –

ENKIDU   What's he at?

HUMBABA's *face changes to something even more dreadful and monstrous, as*
he nurses his anger. He roars, shakes his head from side to side, raises his claws.
GILGAMESH *steps back in some uncertainty.*

HUMBABA
    You will not take me but I will take you.
    I will cast you into the valleys you came through.
    I will break everything, and show your bones
    to my vultures and my eagles, your thrones
    will be void till the end of time –

He makes a sudden lunge at GILGAMESH *and grapples him till he is off*
balance. ENKIDU *springs forward but at first finds it hard to intervene,*
HUMBABA *is so agile and quick and lizard-like in his movements.*
GILGAMESH *and* ENKIDU *both try to reach their weapons, which they*
had laid beside their packs while they went to cut the trees. The three of them
fight grimly, and are frozen in an almost Laocoon-like tableau as a storm brews
over the mountains. The air darkens; mist half blots them out; there is a loud
crack of thunder, which is followed by strong harsh music, leading into the
entrance of SHAMASH *the sun-god, who wears a reversible cloak, gold and*
black, and carries a whip.

SONG OF SHAMASH

    In and out, out and in,
    who will lose and who will win?
    They pray to me but do I care?
    I lash the backsides of the air.
    I have a cloak, a double cloak.
    I turn it this way and they soak
    in streams of gold.
    I turn it that way, they go back
    to fog and cold
    and curse the burden of the black.

40

Now I give my whip a crack:
Southwind, Northwind, Eastwind, Westwind,
Whistling Wind, Piercing Wind, Blizzard Wind, Worst Wind,
Demon Wind, Spirit Wind, Ice Wind, Storm Wind,
and the thirteenth, the sharp Sand-torn Wind,
who will that be lucky for?
and who will bite the rocky floor?
Scry and spell
scry and spell
but I won't tell
no I won't tell.

*Discordant music. Howling of winds. In the darkened air lit by lightning-
flashes,* SHAMASH *vanishes. The trio of* GILGAMESH, ENKIDU, *and*
HUMBABA *comes to life again. The first two manage to reach their weapons,
and in a lull of the storm* HUMBABA *realises that he is dangerously
threatened. His earlier defiance has changed to a plea for mercy.*

HUMBABA
Gilgamesh, king of your people, can we not be friends?
I know you have not come for mercenary ends.
Take away your pointed blade. Such trees
as you need I will help you to cut, ease
your labour, load you with cedar, myrtle, oak,
I have stocks, stacks, go back, reward your folk,
or take me with you as your servant, I
can build your people houses –

ENKIDU
                              Lie after lie!
Gilgamesh, don't be deceived. I know him.
Relax a muscle and you'll end below him
with his fangs in your throat.

HUMBABA
                              I almost had
Gilgamesh there, you scullion, you're mad
to oppose me, I should have snatched you both
at the forest edge, showed you what a Goth
I am, turned your hair white, breathed on you
one torrid toxic blast out of the blue,
fed your curried flesh to the screeching vulture
and the bald eagle. So much for Sumerian culture!

ENKIDU
>Gilgamesh my friend, is that not enough?
>He has tried the smooth, he has tried the rough.
>Make the Guardian of the Cedar Forest
>an ex-guardian, and the trees that have flourished
>here for so many centuries, make them help man.
>No compromise to smother up the plan.
>Kill Humbaba, pulverise him, grind him
>until his very vultures cannot find him!

GILGAMESH
>Humbaba, we must kill you, pulverise you,
>grind you till no vultures recognise you!

HUMBABA (*pointing to* ENKIDU *and uttering a final curse*)
>May he not live the longer of the two.

GILGAMESH *and* ENKIDU *strike* HUMBABA *simultaneously with sword and dagger. They have to strike hard and savagely to penetrate his body armour. He falls, not yet dead.* ENKIDU *holds him down while* GILGAMESH *cuts off his head, to* HUMBABA*'s blood-curdling screams and threshing feet.* GILGAMESH *holds up the head, which drips green blood.* GILGAMESH *and* ENKIDU *look intently at each other. It is a moment of triumph, but tempered by their awareness of* HUMBABA*'s last curse against* ENKIDU. GILGAMESH *sets down the head, which faces the audience. He and* ENKIDU *pick up their axes, go back to the cedar forest, and resume their hacking of the timber. They become shadowy figures, though the sound of the tree-felling is clear. It continues, as a spotlight is thrown on* HUMBABA*'s head.*

END OF ACT TWO

Act Three
Scene One

In the temple. A murmur of conversation. SHAMHAT *and some of her colleagues are sitting around, variously engaged, mending clothes, polishing mirrors, reading clay tablets, etc. One of them points to something in the tablet she is looking at – let us say it is the* Uruk Gazette *– and the others gather round, with a ripple of laughter. A gong sounds loudly, and they stop what they are doing and look up. A* PRIEST *enters, and knocks his staff on the floor.*

PRIEST
> Attention, ladies, for the High Priestess Ishtar!

Enter ISHTAR. *She is a handsome, formidable woman, one of the most important figures in Uruk, accustomed to having her own way. The temple harlots stand and bow.* SHAMHAT, *though a forceful enough person in herself, is respectful in the presence of her mistress (and employer).*

ISHTAR
> Shamhat, I want a word. Things were, things are,
> things will be. Much is to be said and done.

SHAMHAT *gestures to the temple women to leave her and Ishtar alone. They go out.*

> The king has not been in vain to Lebanon.
> We shall have new gates and more, much more.
> What he will be's not what he was before.
> Even those who murmur in the street
> must see it is no game, no parlour feat
> to fight a monster in the frozen north
> and bring us all back something of real worth.
> Shamhat, he goes up in my estimation.
> But yet –

SHAMHAT
>   – but yet, my lady, your hesitation
> suggests the king's new progress is incomplete.

ISHTAR
> Self-love could still become his winding-sheet.
> Lebanon was fine, but he is still alone.

43

It is a simulacrum of a throne.
I must be blunt. What he needs is a queen.

SHAMHAT
Some say he *is* the queen.

ISHTAR
                    It is unclean
even to think so! Shamhat, I am amazed.
He is a lion, a bull. He has been praised
for his strength by poets far and wide. No no,
you are off the mark. He is a tower. Go
to the soldiers, go to the huntsmen, they
will tell you no less limp wrist ever saw day.

SHAMHAT
I only said 'some say'. He has his enemies.

ISHTAR
So have all who reach such eminence.
He is a man of men, and needs a queen.
Only one cloud lurks in this clear scene –

SHAMHAT
The cloud that occupies the twin throne?

ISHTAR
                            Indeed.
Tell me about Enkidu. Can you read
his soul as I know you have read his flesh,
that is to say, closely?

SHAMHAT
                    Innocent, fresh,
impressionable, confused, civilised more or less,
he's gained a palace, lost a wilderness.
Not really lost; he carries it within.
A natural man, one toe in our lake of sin.

ISHTAR
Speak for yourself, Shamhat. Uruk is holy,
watched by many gods. Wildness is folly.
Strip Enkidu's veneer –

SHAMHAT
                              – and you will find
    the goodness of a natural heart.

ISHTAR
                              Too kind,
    too kind. He has taken half the throne.
    Ambition will not stop at being half-grown.

SHAMHAT
    You wrong him, my lady. He is totally devoted
    to curbing powers on which the king has doted
    too long.

ISHTAR
                    Shamhat, these words are dangerous.
    The powers are on tiptoe to favour us
    if we stand firm for what we know is best.
    Enkidu must be shouldered from the nest.

SHAMHAT
    Gain that, Ishtar, and you may lose the rest.

ISHTAR *glares angrily at her, claps her hands. The* PRIEST *reappears and
ushers her out.* SHAMHAT *bows.*

Scene Two

A room in the palace. GILGAMESH *is freshening up after his successful
Lebanese expedition. Servants, including his* MAJOR-DOMO *and the royal*
BARBER, *are looking after him with some excitement and admiration, talking
quietly, laying out new clothes, etc. The* BARBER *is preparing to wash his
hair.*

BARBER
    Never seen such hair, sir, where has it been?
    It was always long, but this – really – I mean –
    I've seen a stork's nest on a palace chimney –
    it's *matted thick*, I'll have to use my thingmy –
    (*he rummages for a special comb*)
    now sir, this will *tug*, but bear with me –

45

The king winces, but is in indulgent and happy mood.

> I think we're ready to wash – I'll let you see
> and smell – here – our new Egyptian soap
> or *savon* – quite terrific – it can cope
> (*he washes the king's hair vigorously*)
> with the most difficult cases. I haven't seen
> Egypt, have you, sir?

The king mutters something.

> You have to be keen
> on death, I understand. Mummies of cats.
> Granny on the shelf. Really I think that's
> too much. – Last rinse sir, then the fan.
> I've taken out a patent. Ratchets, a han-
> dle, I turn, hot air comes out and blows
> your majesty's luxuriance into flows
> and waves like the Euphrates. Poetry.
> Right down your back, sir, shake it free.
> The crown will hold it in place. You see?

BARBER *holds up metal mirror.* GILGAMESH *nods, stands, stretches, ready to be dressed. Servants come forward with fresh colourful robes, which they put on the king. There is a broad belt, which he buckles himself. Finally he sets the crown on his head, as the mirror is again held up for him. He beams. He is ready for anything. The* BARBER *exits with his paraphernalia. Suddenly a trumpet sounds outside the palace, with a distinctive note which everyone recognises. The servants whisper 'It's Ishtar!', 'The High Priestess!', 'Ishtar!'. The* MAJOR-DOMO *motions the servants to one side, sets himself in front of the king, and faces towards the entrance to the room, where a small but impressive procession slowly approaches. Erotic music. Priests, eunuchs, temple harlots, and lastly* ISHTAR *and her bodyguards, come onstage.* ISHTAR *is regally dressed for the occasion. She has carefully chosen a moment when Enkidu is absent. The* MAJOR-DOMO *and the leading* PRIEST *stand forward from opposite sides.*

MAJOR-DOMO
> To be honoured by a visit leaves still a query.
> What would you have of us here, sacred equerry?

PRIEST
> My mistress Ishtar, divine in love and power,
> seeks Gilgamesh at (we hope) a propitious hour.

46

MAJOR-DOMO
Fully to identify the propitiousness:
the nature of this brilliant mission is – ?

PRIEST
Intermediaries cannot privilege secrecy;
my lady's propositions are hers to essay.

MAJOR-DOMO
A proposition makes a pregnant meeting.
Let Ishtar be about her bush, no beating.

PRIEST
Ishtar's honey flows at its own rate,
but she will not resile or equivocate.

The two men bow stiffly to each other, and move back. ISHTAR *and*
GILGAMESH *come forward till they are face to face. A subdued buzz among
their respective retinues falls silent as* ISHTAR *begins to speak.*

ISHTAR
Gilgamesh, lord of Uruk, master of cedars,
tiresome to add 'one of the world's leaders'
but the cliché is true: your last exploits
make city life tame as a game of quoits.
I exaggerate, but as part of your praise;
you spread the sense of half-fulfilled days.
Yet you yourself are surely unfulfilled.
You are like a flash coin still unmilled.
You have wealth, power, you are a man of men,
lions are wary of you. Why then
do you sleep alone, with only a senseless sheet
covering your wasted treasures? Here we meet
as equals, Gilgamesh, unguarded as life.
My words are unguarded: let me be your wife.

Whispered buzz from the two retinues. GILGAMESH *looks startled and is
about to speak, but she continues:*

Hear me out, Gilgamesh. Let me be free
with you. In Sumer, there is a great tree
reaching into the blue. That tree is you.
I want your luscious fruits. Nothing will do
but I must climb and press that lusciousness.

47

Pomegranates of fire, peaches of pure sense!

There is a reaction in both retinues to her outspoken sensuality. But she is
wound up now, and nothing can stop her.

But what have I to give you in return?
A million things are waiting in their turn!
I have the wealth behind my temple walls
to make your coffers tawdry market-stalls.
You need a chariot? I'll have one made
of gold and lapis-lazuli, highest grade,
even the wheels will be gold, and the fierce horns
will shine in silver-gold electrum; storms
of dust will rise as you ride and command
great mountain mules I'll harness for your hand.
Come into our house and smell the cedarwood,
is it not sweet? And do you not find it good
when you come in, that door and throne bow down
to kiss your feet? Nothing cannot be done.
Your footstools can be kings, princes, lords.
Gypsies will bring you brimming tribute-hoards
of berry and vine from hidden field and hill.
Your she-goats will have triplets, your ewes fill
pastures with twins, your poor draught donkey run
to overtake the mule, your yoked ox in the sun
priceless, peerless, your chariot-horse keen,
bristling, pawing, snorting to conquer the scene –

GILGAMESH
What scene? What scenario? What is this aria?
A charabanc to a charivari, hah?
What would you need from me if I married you?
Oil, meat, clothes, wine, if I carried you
over the threshold? Or my life, my pith, my wit,
my very self? Would you let me stand, or sit,
or only lie, and lie, all ways, to be sucked dry?
I know you, Ishtar, as the passers-by
know you, haunting the lanes, waiting for men.
Schizophrenic queen of harlots, the pen
that cut your clay was not the king of heaven
as you love to claim, but a demon driven
down into lust like a butter-knife, dripping
erect with a toss of trustless glamour. Stripping
your rhetoric gives me the greatest pleasure.

ISHTAR angrily *moves forward to interrupt, but* GILGAMESH *threatens his very strong right arm, and continues:*

No, it is my turn now, and for good measure
I must remind those present, of your past.
You are an oven where foolish ice can't last,
a half-door that lets in every draught,
a murderous palace where soldiers fought and laughed,
an elephant that eats its own howdah,
a ball of pitch that blackens every handler,
a waterskin that leaks and soaks its carrier,
a limestone warp that loosens the firm barrier,
a battering-ram that lets the enemy in,
a shoe that bites the feet and bares the skin.
Where are the bridegrooms that you kept for ever?
Where is Tammuz your very first lover?
You had the nerve to order laments for him
each year, your victim, sweet songs and scents for him.
You loved that brilliant bird the shepherds love,
but smashed his wing; what can he sing of
now as he stands in the forest but 'My wing!'
You loved the lion, the lion who is king,
and yet you dug his death pits, seven, seven again.
You loved the battle-hungry stallion, then
unloved him with whips and goads, made him
gallop seven hours and seven, to degrade him
at last as he drank deep from a muddied lake,
made his mother wail comfortless for his sake.
You loved the master shepherd who baked your bread
and killed a kid for you; hit him half-dead
and turned him into a wolf: his shepherds, his dogs
chase him to misery. And that gardener in his clogs,
your father's man, who brought you daily flowers
and glistening baskets of dates, you used your powers,
looked at him, came close, asked for his hairy hand
to stroke your cunt, that well-split date –

ISHTAR cries out, flies towards GILGAMESH *to attack him, and is restrained by her followers.* GILGAMESH *continues, with emphasis:*

                              – and, and
how humiliated you were when he said no,
Ishtar-would-be-Chatterley, felled him with a blow,
turned the gardener into a gnome, fixed him,

let his Eden go waste and eighty-sixed him.
You think I'd marry you? You must be mad.
I'd sooner spend the night in Bluebeard's pad!

General consternation. Some cheers from GILGAMESH's *retinue, howls and curses from* ISHTAR's *retinue. She herself sobs and cries bitterly at her public humiliation, but is strong enough, before she is swept offstage, protected by her followers, to say:*

ISHTAR
You will be sorry, Gilgamesh! I swear
the gods I serve will strip your glory bare!

GILGAMESH *waves her roughly away, as she exits with her followers. He seems unperturbed, though some of his retinue are whispering and shaking their heads as they watch* ISHTAR *depart.*

Scene Three

ISHTAR's *own room in the temple. A brazier with incense.* ISHTAR *is calling loudly on* ANU, *the father of the gods, to listen to her complaint about* GILGAMESH.

ISHTAR
Anu, father of the gods, king of the sky,
your faithful priestess and daughter utters a cry
against Gilgamesh who has insulted her honour,
regaling Uruk with slanders and throwing upon her
a cloak of mud which clings and stings. Destroy him
I beg of you, great father, let hell enjoy him.
Great king, put down this despicable king!
Take from him what he has, take everything!

ANU *materialises in a corner of the room. As the chief deity in the Sumerian pantheon (who appears again later on) he should look quite impressive, and not some doddery Jehovah or Blakean Nobodaddy. As the primeval sky-god, he would have blue and silver as his colours.*

ANU
Ishtar, Ishtar, as you see, we heard you in heaven.
What a jangle! Are you really so rent and riven?

50

ISHTAR

    Lord Anu, he fastened on me a vile history.
    He gave me lusts that soiled my ministry.

ANU

    Surely he must have been the provocatee?

ISHTAR

    I only asked the man to marry me.

ANU (*laughs*)

    I cannot just quite see you as a wife.

ISHTAR

    There are wives and wives. He would add to my life
    the power of his kingdom and his body.
    Making a fire in winter in his study,
    laying out his Persian slippers – no thanks.
    I leave such details to the lower ranks.

ANU

    Do you love him?

ISHTAR

                  I love his physical equipment.

ANU

    Hate him?

ISHTAR

                I want revenge, by the next shipment.

ANU

    So what do you want shipped?

ISHTAR

                     The Bull of Heaven.

ANU

    This is a desperate method to get even.
    The Bull of Heaven is a last resort.
    Annihilating harvests is his sport.
    Scorched earth, terror, burials follow him.

ISHTAR
I want him. Round him up and collar him.
Uruk has barns and silos stuffed with grain.
Our mortuaries can take five hundred slain.
If Gilgamesh is one, that makes my day.

ANU
Ishtar, you should be careful what you pray.
Those who get what they pestered heaven for
can buy wersh bread God had no leaven for.

ISHTAR
I'll take that risk. The Bull, Anu, the Bull!
When I hear its brazen roar, my cup is full!
So be it. I have said what I have said.

ANU *fades away.* ISHTAR *lifts her arms to heaven in a gesture of triumph.*

ISHTAR
The king who would not wed will soon be dead.

Scene Four

*The market-square. Citizens strolling about, talking, shopping. Street buskers
are playing instruments, juggling, etc. Suddenly there is a distant drumming
sound. People pause, listen, but then go back to their business as the noise stops.
But after a few moments it starts up again, nearer and louder, and accompanied
by a great bellow. There is still nothing to be seen, but the crowds are now
thoroughly disturbed and apprehensive, staring in the direction of the sound. At
last the* BULL OF HEAVEN *appears. Although from one point of view it is a
supernatural creature sent by Anu to punish Gilgamesh, it is also a real large
black bull, with wings, huge horns, and a nose-ring. It trots angrily into the
square, bellowing and slavering lavishly at one end and shitting lavishly at the
other. (So says the original poem, but the director can omit the latter if it is felt
to be too problematic! It is however a good example of the poem's range of tone,
from the exalted to the coarse. Gilgamesh's Sumerian pun on date / cunt in Act
3 Scene 2 is another instance.) People scatter in panic. The bull, roaring and
snorting, is quick on its feet and tramples and gores some of the citizens. Cries
and shrieks everywhere. One citizen runs to the palace entrance and shouts for*
GILGAMESH *and* ENKIDU. *They emerge hurrying to size up the*

52

situation. They notice ISHTAR *standing high and safe on the wall of the temple, avidly taking in the scene, and they guess what she is up to.* ENKIDU *has a dagger in his belt and* GILGAMESH *has a sword.*

ENKIDU

    The Bull of Heaven! Ishtar has wheedled God
    to give her the Bull of Heaven. She wants a rod
    to break your back because you shamed her.

GILGAMESH

                                  Two horns
    and four legs sent from heaven or hell: she scorns
    a simple rod! Tanks and flamethrowers
    lurk in that hide. But we can be sowers
    of death as well as any beast. Watch out!

The BULL OF HEAVEN, *scenting two new enemies, has come thundering up towards the palace.*

    The tail! Torment and twist his tail! I'll clout
    his nose-ring, make him mad and careless. He's
    bursting with unearthly hatred and sleaze –
    typical Ishtar golem.

ENKIDU

                  Programmed for you.

GILGAMESH

    Programmed for both of us. Quick now – screw!

ENKIDU *has manoeuvred himself to the back of the bull and seized the ragged filthy tail. He twists it hard till the animal bellows in pain and swivels round to attack him. He leaps aside and comes to the front. As he does so, the bull hurls him against the wall and tries to crush him.*

ENKIDU

    Gilgamesh! I can't breathe!

GILGAMESH

                I'll draw him from you.
    He's strong, I'm stronger. Hell shall never storm you.

GILGAMESH *grips the horns of the bull with both hands and wrenches the head this way and that. The bull roars and moves away from* ENKIDU, *who runs to help* GILGAMESH. *The fight drags them across the stage, away from the palace.*

GILGAMESH
Take the horns, hold them, hold them tight, tight.
I'll draw my sword and put this soul to flight.

ENKIDU
What soul? It's a construct. It's not real.

GILGAMESH
I'll give it death. Don't tell me it can't feel.

While ENKIDU *clutches the horns,* GILGAMESH *lifts his sword, gropes with one hand for the fatal spot between nape and shoulders, and plunges the blade deeply into the bull. The bull gives a low fearsome groan as it slowly sinks to its knees and finally keels over, dead.* GILGAMESH *withdraws the sword and holds it up to* ISHTAR *with a shout of triumph. His other arm embraces* ENKIDU's *shoulders.*

ISHTAR
May no good come to Gilgamesh, who slew
the Bull of Heaven and ran my good name through!

ENKIDU, *enraged by her cursing of his friend, hacks off a slice from the bull's hindquarters and throws it at her, accurately, so that the meat hits her on the face. As she shrieks, he cries out:*

ENKIDU
If I could get at you I would kill you too –
hang you in the bull's intestines!

ISHTAR *disappears into the temple, wailing.*

GILGAMESH
                                        Enkidu:
look here. You were right. It's not a bull
but a bovoid, a replicant. Look: pull.
When is a horn not a horn? When you can see
it's specially hardened lapis-lazuli.
We shall have drinking-horns from these, and toast
the day when Ishtar copped her rawest roast!

The citizens are removing the dead and tending to the injured. They cast horrified or angry glances at the carcase of the bull, but do not approach it. One of them brings a bowl of water for GILGAMESH *and* ENKIDU *to wash their hands, which they do. Then the two men, dishevelled as they are, stride through the street towards the palace, 'hand in hand' (see previous comment on this), in happy and boastful mood, too full of themselves to notice that the populace are mostly staring at them, with only a few cheering or clapping.*

THE SONG OF TRIUMPH OF GILGAMESH

Who is the bravest of the men?
Who is the boldest of the males?
Gilgamesh is the bravest of the men.
Gilgamesh is the boldest of the males.
Who is the best of the friends?
Who is the crystal of the companions?
Enkidu is the best of the friends.
Enkidu is the crystal of the companions.
And who is the worst of the women?
And who is the leeriest of the lovers?
Ishtar is the worst of the women.
Ishtar is the leeriest of the lovers.

GILGAMESH
Tonight I open the palace to a celebration.
All are welcome on this auspicious occasion.

Scene Five

Night. Lamps. A room in the palace. Long table with guests, including the JESTER. GILGAMESH *and* ENKIDU *sit side by side. The feast in celebration of the killing of the bull has been in full swing for some time, and has reached the noisy stage. The wine has been flowing, and servants are still assiduously circulating with large jugs. A small band plays in one corner.*

1ST GUEST
Enkidu, why did you throw the bull's arse at her
and not its pizzle?

ENKIDU (*embarrassed*)
            I was no arbiter

of such niceties. There was no time for symbolism.

2ND GUEST
Maybe he thought a last shot of hot jism
would be too near the bone. For him, I mean.

3RD GUEST
How's Shamhat these days anyway? A queen
of pros. Great girl. Do you see her still?

GILGAMESH (*interrupting a dangerous turn in the conversation*)
That's in the past. Relax and drink your fill.
We've meat, wealth, shelter, wine, and a dead bull.
The music and the night are beautiful.

1ST GUEST (*determined to stir things up somehow*)
The Jester is unusually abstemious.
Is he afraid to let off steam at us?

GUESTS
Come on the Jester! – Tell us a story! – The Jester!

JESTER (*stands up, looks round company, lifts drum from floor and gives it a roll*)
If thae music-makers wid jist turn the volume doon a bit – ta – Ah'll tell yese a wee storyette. Wance upon a time – an it wiz wanst, only wanst, no twicet or thricet or any other thing, so dinny think it – wance upon a time therr wiz a Sultan in Samarkand, which Ah canny say wherr it is yit, since it's still in the future – wance therr wiz this Sultan an he wiz oot watterin his gairden wae a nice big watterin-can, when whit diz he see but a bonny-like lassie staunin unner a tree sayin she wiz the Queen o the Fairies or some such stupit thing an that she hud a lovely wee bush of her ain, in her ain gairden, an wid he come wae his fine big watterin-can an gie her bush a sprinkle. Naw naw, says the Sultan, Ah'm sorry ma dear, but Ah've gote tae gie ma pet cheetah a dauner an a run, an Ah've nae time tae go tae Fairyland. The Fairy wisny exackly pleased at this answer, an sayed sumhm like 'Cheeta bateeta abrakabaleesta!', which the Sultan took tae be some kinna spell, but anywey away he went an walked his cheetah. Well, so that wiz orright, but then a few weeks eftir this, the Sultan thought his cheetah wiz gettin gey thin, an hud mair spotes than it hud before, so he telt the best vet in Samarkand tae come an take a shufti at the poor beast, an the vet shook his heid an sayed naethin wid save the cheetah except the root of a wee bush that grew in Fairyland. So that Sultan, that Sultan gaed

white as a sheet an felt a stoond at his hert, for he kent therr wizz nae
saicont chance tae get tae Fairyland in this life. – That's it, folks. Ah'll
huv a wee refreshment noo.

The JESTER *bangs his drum and sits down. He is poured a large drink, and
swallows it with relish.*

1ST GUEST
That's crap. There's no such place as Fairyland.

2ND GUEST
And anyway, where the hell is Samarkand?

3RD GUEST
I thought this was meant to be a celebration!

GILGAMESH
A cautionary tale fits any occasion.

ENKIDU
The Sultan leaves us much for rumination.

1ST GUEST
Still ruminant? Too much bull. It's a fixation.

ENKIDU (*laughs*)
Not a bit of it! Drink, drink up, my friends!
The feast is wearing to its candle-ends.
We cannot see it, but beyond these walls
the goddess of the moon rides waterfalls
of brilliant silver onto our terraces
and brings the universe held in her tresses
of stars down here among us. On our roof-tiles
astronomers pace out imaginary miles –
hundreds, thousands? – into the darkness; they say
we are ourselves a part of the Milky Way.
If this is not greatness, what is it?
We belong to a destiny, not a visit.
I think we should be happy; we are meant to;
it is not heaven or hell that we were sent to
but this green earth so drenched in blood and tears
that it has got to bear such fruit, vines, ears
as the unpeopled galaxies cannot know.
Tomorrow, someday, Shamash will make it so.

Friends – Gilgamesh – Jester – I've rambled on.
The wine has played its piece. Some carillon!
In vino veritas, as the Hittites say.
Forgive me if I'm out of order! Today –
for it's past midnight – let us crown the feast
with a last dance in honour of the east
where light and life will soon be dancing too!

GILGAMESH
A perfect ending! If this was Xanadu
we'd have a pleasure-dome, a mirror-ball,
who knows what else, but here we have on call
goodwill, good fellowship, victorious souls
and those who love victorious souls. The Bulls
of Heaven may come and go, *will* come and go,
but there are still great powers here below.
Ishtar mourns in her tower. I scattered her vengeance
like dust, Enkidu at my side. The engines
of Anu ceased to roar. Our anger was sated.

1ST GUEST
The dead and wounded – ?

GILGAMESH
                        – will be compensated.
A little money clears us of this deed.
But now let us take the floor with ready speed,
before the first grey kills the astronomer's sky.
Let's move, let's dance. We've drained the flagons dry!

The table is drawn to one side to clear a dancing-space. The band prepares for a new, strongly rhythmic, upbeat number. The feasters are not drunk, but have fed and imbibed well and are happy and positive, with loosened inhibitions. The dance can be as strange as the director likes, given the ancient and exotic setting, but it should be of a formal type, not chaotic or sloppy – a sort of controlled wildness, perhaps, such as you get in some Scottish country dancing. Partners should be exchanged, with a mixing of genders. The total effect should be as a triumphant conclusion to the day's actions, as far as GILGAMESH *and* ENKIDU *are concerned, despite any shadow that may have been cast by the* JESTER's *story, and despite the less than wholehearted enthusiasm of the populace, some of whom have joined the celebration while others have stayed at home. It is the highest point in the trajectory of* GILGAMESH *and* ENKIDU, *from which the future can only provide a descent. The music should stop abruptly, on a loud note, and not fade away gradually or quietly. As it stops, the dancers realise the evening is over, and the guests make their goodbyes and exeunt, as the band also pack up their instruments and leave. Last to go is the* JESTER, *whose one (long) drink has proved rather strong for him.*

JESTER

Hasta la vista, as the Bedouin say. *Hasta la vista*, Gilgameshuggenah, king, sur, majesty an at. *Hasta la vista*, Enkidoolally, king, sur, majesty an at. Ye're a daft perr, but Ah'm no gaun tae knock ye. Sumdy else'll dae that, nae doot. G'night, g'moarnin, g'day.

JESTER *bangs drum uncertainly and exits on not entirely steady feet.* GILGAMESH *and* ENKIDU, *alone at last, sweating and glistening from the dancing and drinking, stand facing each other, silently but intently, for quite a few seconds. Then* GILGAMESH *takes* ENKIDU *by the hand (no doubt about it this time), and they walk slowly to the back of the stage (backs to audience), where a curtain is drawn to reveal a bedroom – with one bed. Gradual blackout as they move towards the bed.*

END OF ACT THREE

Act Four
Scene One

In heaven. ANU *the sky-god and* SHAMASH *the sun-god are debating the future of* GILGAMESH *and* ENKIDU.

ANU
    We must go over the matter part by part.
    No one will stand on clouds and throw a dart.
    If crisis there is, and I must believe it,
    we do not flail around and later grieve it.
    Wrongs have been done that cannot be rescinded,
    but even if the harmonies are winded
    they must regain their breath, and speak.

SHAMASH
                               Anu,
    nothing that happens is ever out of view
    to those who watch. I circle what circles me.
    The lightning is not mine that kills the tree.

ANU
    You think it's mine? a naive Jovian bolt?
    You saw me holstering my smoking Colt?
    No no, if we say things must come to pass
    or must not come to pass, the critical mass
    will stir or not stir not by my command
    but through what even I don't understand.

SHAMASH
    You go beyond me. Aren't we here to decide
    whether two kings can still sit side by side?

ANU
    My feeling is that one of them must die.
    What think you, Shamash?

SHAMASH
                    I can hardly deny
    that they have gone too far. They killed the guardian
    of Lebanon in his giant sacred garden
    of cedars, and chopped down the indignant wood –

ANU

    – doubling their misdemeanour with a crude
    and violent execution of the Bull
    of Heaven –

SHAMASH

        – and then so arrogant and cool
    you'd think they had forgotten our existence –

ANU

    – and thus forgotten our infinite persistence
    to make men feel as they never felt before.

SHAMASH

    So pain and sorrow, of which we have great store,
    must be encouraged to descend –

ANU

                Shamash,
    not only pain and sorrow, but the brash
    knock of death must be heard. Let the gate
    of cedar, new as it is, creak out the fate
    of its high thief.

SHAMASH

        Thieves.

ANU

           All right, but who
    had the greater guilt, who but Enkidu?
    Why should a woodsman hunt the divine protector
    of the greatest woods in the world? It is a spectre,
    that betrayal – and he knew it – that haunts my mind.

SHAMASH

    And yet Humbaba's beheading was assigned
    to Gilgamesh. He exulted.

ANU

           They both exulted.
    But Humbaba was more unforgivably insulted
    by a turncoat townee who fought on the wrong side.
    You are soft on Enkidu because he deified –
    if that's the word – the natural power you foment,

and threw at you his naive temperament.

SHAMASH

Yet you are soft on Gilgamesh, though he
insulted Ishtar, your dubious devotee.

ANU

I am not soft on anyone. I have plans
for Gilgamesh. I await circumstance.
It may have been an infamous rejection –

SHAMASH

– with quite a few home truths in his dissection –

ANU

– but the king's scorn was of a recent date:
why want a wife when you have gained a mate?

SHAMASH

So everything comes back to Enkidu?
Wrapping the king in spells, shining with dew,
stopping heredity with animal cries?

ANU

It is for men, not gods, to theorise.

SHAMASH

Gilgamesh matadored the Bull of Heaven.

ANU

Enkidu held the horns. That makes them even.

SHAMASH

When did Enkidu lift men off the streets?

ANU

That is another matter. There are no retreats.
My tablets are gouged deep with the king's deeds.
There are things to come. I know what pleads, what bleeds.

SHAMASH

If that is so, I am content.

ANU

Let us

make sure Enkidu is prepared. His debt is
to be paid in human terms, not ours.
His sickness begins –

SHAMASH

now –

ANU

and for hours –

SHAMASH
 – and days –

ANU

less than two weeks –

SHAMASH

he lies
in pain of mind and body. I shall advise
Enkidu in a dream that he must die,
and give time for that wild soul not to defy
but take what he cannot escape. It is hard.

ANU
It is what happens.

SHAMASH

To men, it may be hard.

Scene Two

A room in the palace. Night. A lamp. A chair and a small table. The room has
a window. GILGAMESH *is talking to a* DOCTOR *who has his bag beside*
him. ENKIDU *lies on a bed, where he has been examined by the* DOCTOR.

DOCTOR
How long has he been like this?

GILGAMESH
 Ten days

or thereabouts, most sudden of decays
yet seemingly relentless, a mere weakness
at first, a stumble or two, until the sickness
(whatever it is) got hold. Lethargy punctuated
by fever. Terrible night sweats. I've waited
beside his soaking pillow to hear visions,
groans, half-comprehensible derisions,
and then a racking cough as dry as straw.

DOCTOR

I cannot see a cure on which to draw.
The case is strange, not like any other.

GILGAMESH

Do it, doctor. You are well paid. Cure my brother!

The DOCTOR *takes a small bottle of medicine from his bag and hands it to*
GILGAMESH.

DOCTOR

This should reduce the fever. Let me know
of any change, my lord. Now I must go.

The DOCTOR *bows to* GILGAMESH *and exits.* ENKIDU, *tossing and
turning on the bed, suddenly wakes up with a shout and sits up.*

ENKIDU

Gilgamesh!

GILGAMESH *comes over.*

Oh Gilgamesh, I had a dream,
a nightmare! Who sends these things? I seem
to be marked out for death, that's it, for dying.
I looked up at the sky and the sun, trying
to hear words on the wind, gods on the wing,
and all I heard was 'Death!', then nothing, nothing!
Oh Gilgamesh, what is wrong with me? Why
do I have to leave you, why do I have to die?

GILGAMESH

Gods, dear gods, if you exist, what is it
you want, or need, will you not visit
your anger on me, and save my dearest friend.

What has he done that I have not done? Bend
the bow on me! He is too young for the Shades!

ENKIDU

Oh the chill, the heat! Whatever it is that invades
my body – fire, lead, ice – is in too far
to be routed, I feel it, I feel my star
is setting. Is the sun a star? Oh Shamash,
I know you could burn the whole world to ash.
Am I worth your displeasure?

GILGAMESH (*offers the* DOCTOR's *phial*)
                              Here, drink this,
the doctor left it.

ENKIDU
                              I don't want it. What bliss
to throw it at the gate and poison it,
the Cedar Gate, give it a deadly hit
with your old pointy-hat charlatan's ampoules,
that cursèd wood which we brought down in armfuls
from the cursèd forest –

GILGAMESH
                              Don't, Enkidu, don't!
There is no sense in what you are saying. You won't
kill your fever with words –

ENKIDU
                              Dumb, senseless gate,
you are too stupid even to prevaricate.
You stand there smug and sound and stiff and sure.
I picked you out with care on that adventure,
pieces of the best, weather-resistant,
posts and jambs and panels all consistent,
I saw it in my mind's eye in Lebanon
and brought it back like Frankenstein. Undone
I am by you, monstrous faithless construction,
I gave you life, you give me my destruction!
If I had known what you would do to me,
I would have cast those cedars in the sea!
May you be rubbished by some later king.
The dying scorpion leaves you this sting.

GILGAMESH
    A stock of timber, a thing of hinges? My friend,
    this is madness. You cannot blame the bend
    in the river for an oxbow ambush. The gate
    stands, it is ours, it is Uruk's. If fate
    seems vicious, you must not be. Think the best,
    never the worst. It is late. Try to rest.

ENKIDU *subsides into the pillows, muttering, exhausted. He falls into an uneasy sleep.* GILGAMESH *sits in a chair at the bedside, sometimes gazing at him anxiously, sometimes nodding off and waking with a start. He occasionally wipes* ENKIDU's *face with a cloth. He prowls round the room to keep awake, returns to the chair again. The room slowly grows lighter, until a cock crows somewhere in the distance and as the morning sunlight streams in through the window,* GILGAMESH *covers the lamp, and after a last look at the sleeping* ENKIDU, *exits quietly from the room. After a short interval, two* NURSES *enter with basin of water and towels. They wake* ENKIDU *with 'Good-morning, Lord Enkidu!', 'It is a fine day', etc. as they lift and prop him up, take off his sweat-soaked nightshirt, give him a brief wash and a new garment to wear, and tidy up his bed. One of them exits and immediately brings back a bowl of soup.* ENKIDU, *though more calm than he was on the previous night, is still shaky, and rattles the spoon against the bowl as he manages to sup. (His calm, however, is soon to be tested and shaken.) Finally the* NURSES *put the half-finished bowl on the bedside table, together with a new vase of flowers which one of them brings in, and an inscribed clay tablet for* ENKIDU *to read if he feels like it.* ENKIDU *says nothing, but patiently accepts their ministrations. He stares into space as they leave. When they are almost offstage, the* MAJOR-DOMO *enters and whispers some message to them. They look back at* ENKIDU *and shake their heads doubtfully. The* MAJOR-DOMO *appears to insist, dismisses them, and walks into the room, coughing lightly to announce his presence to the sick man, and gently tapping with his staff.*

MAJOR-DOMO
    Forgive me for intruding, Lord Enkidu,
    I have two visitors who ask to see you.

ENKIDU (*coughs, then*)
    Who?

MAJOR-DOMO
        The trapper Nedu, the harlot Shamhat.

ENKIDU (*much agitated, raising himself in the bed, speaking with a dangerous edge to his voice*)
    Let them come in, god, yes, let them dare that.

The MAJOR-DOMO *bows, exits, comes back with* NEDU *and*
SHAMHAT, *who stand a little uncertainly near the bed. The* MAJOR-
DOMO *is unobtrusively in the background during remainder of scene.*

NEDU

My lord, Uruk grieves for your sickness. I came
to pay my respects. I think you know my name.

ENKIDU

Nedu, I know and remember you. I see
you have come to gloat over my misery.
When I was one with nature, you slunk and plotted
to splice me away and make me all besotted
with the silk and filth of cities, to my confusion
as you will know, and to my dissolution
as you now see. What do you want of me?

NEDU

Nothing, except your health. Could I foresee
what the hard stars had in store for you?
We all believed life could do more for you
than run with deer and sink your teeth in roots.
Cooked versus raw? Are these your mental fruits?

ENKIDU

You never wanted anything for me.
You wanted something for the state. Agree!

NEDU

My lord –

ENKIDU

You used me, is all. You used me.

NEDU

I tried –

ENKIDU

No, you succeeded. The gods have accused me
of sins I never knew before you took me
out of the forest. Demons have come to hook me –
(*He is racked by a fit of coughing*)
little barbs deep in my throat, behind my eyes,
but not so that I cannot recognise

67

the instigator of my pain. The dying
are allowed three curses. I've sent one flying,
have two left in my quiver. May you, Nedu,
find your traps sprung empty that once fed you,
and may your chaffering fall on deaf ears,
and may your golden profits be arrears,
and may you enter the house of destitution
and pray in vain for days of restitution.

ENKIDU's *anger is really a kind of despair, and it has carried him away into
an abstract prophetic area. He does not even look at the trapper as he utters his
curse.* The MAJOR-DOMO *comes forward to speak to the bewildered
trapper.*

MAJOR-DOMO
Best to leave, sir. It is his sickness speaks.

NEDU
What I did was for the best.

MAJOR-DOMO
He seeks
release from pain of mind as well as body.
He would be the same with anybody.

NEDU *exits.* SHAMHAT *trembles, but addresses* ENKIDU.

SHAMHAT
Dear Lord Enkidu, hear me when I say
it kills me to have to see you in this way.
We have been close –

ENKIDU
Close as a clam's lips.
That time is silent. By the curve of your hips
I think you would start it all over again.
You are the painted pit that gapes for men,
lubricious Corrievreckan that sucks and sucks
and drowns the pith of things even as it fucks.

SHAMHAT
Enkidu, in our seven nights together
I never heard or felt you wonder whether
all was not well. We were as one.

68

ENKIDU

                    One blot,
one error, one dungeon, one burning pot
of unfulfillable desires, one web
that mazed and trussed me at the semen's ebb.
You betrayed me to power, you set me
on a scalding throne and it will never let me
escape the racing fevers and fibres – my veins –
ah but I am on fire – all these lit trains
of powder, skeins of acid –

He threshes about in a quick but brief fever-fit. SHAMHAT *moves closer to help him, but he recovers and rebuffs her.*

                    Keep away!
I have one curse left, one skin to flay.
May you never make yourself house or home
or be able to bear a child to call your own.
May the temple harlots write you off the map.
May beer-dregs slither down your lovely lap
and drunkards lace your festive robe with sick.
May potters throw you nothing but burnt brick.
May you only window-shop for alabaster.
May the judge sneer and ask, Who is your master?
May your house have no delectable silver to shine
because in fact you have no house, but go
about your business at close and cul-de-sac.
May a wasteland be your sleeping-place, and the black
of city walls your known and lonely stand.
May thorns and briars draw blood. May the hard hand
of drunk and sober clients hit your cheek,
when your disgusting cunt begins to leak.
For you have brought everything against me,
used and abused and utterly un-sensed me.

SHAMHAT *bursts out crying and falls to her knees with her arms over the foot of the bed.*

SHAMHAT

It is not true! I loved you, and still do.
What have the gods done to us, Enkidu?

ENKIDU, *who has worked himself up into a near-frenzy, stares at her, then raises his arms and head to heaven.*

ENKIDU

    We shall find out. Shamash! Shamash! Shamash!

SHAMASH *the sun-god materialises in bright yellow light.* *The* MAJOR-
DOMO *falls to his knees.*

SHAMASH

    Enkidu, why do you put this harlot under the lash?
    Who gave you your first bread to taste? Who poured
    your first wine? Who dressed you like a lord?
    Who put the beauty of Gilgamesh in your hands?
    Your love for your friend will be known in all lands.
    Your brother made you lie on the couch of honour,
    the couch of greatness. It was a high wonder
    to the world when you sat at his left side
    and princes kissed your feet. Once you have died,
    the people will weep for you with public clamour.
    Praise Shamhat! Praise her love and praise her glamour!

ENKIDU, *chastened and sobered by the sun-god's words, finds his anger has
drained away, and sees* SHAMHAT *and her suffering as if for the first time.*

ENKIDU

    Come, Shamhat, no more curses, let me bless you.
    The demon in my blood could only address you
    from its black heart of pain. God knows I'm not
    the madman I must have seemed. It's not a lot
    of time I have to ask forgiveness, but I do,
    and every badness that I laid on you
    I annul. May those of power and fame
    love you. May one still miles away untame
    his hair in the wind, riding in anticipation.
    May the soldier always welcome your invitation,
    unbuckle his belt for you, give you such things
    as he has won in war, filigree earrings,
    lapis-lazuli, rock-crystal images and gold,
    may he heap your lap with what campaigns have rolled
    into his pack. May the wife, although a mother
    of seven, be abandoned for no other
    than you!

SHAMASH

           Now you have made amends, Enkidu.
    You must be firm. What is to come for you

will not be without pain. It must be borne.
The veil trembles, it is nearly torn.

SHAMASH *slowly disappears.*

SHAMHAT
    Enkidu, anything I can do or say
    to solace you is yours to command, today,
    tomorrow, any day. Gods come and go,
    but you will never find me loath or slow.

The MAJOR-DOMO *comes forward to beckon her away, and leave*
ENKIDU *to get some rest.* ENKIDU *stares at her with a mixed, vulnerable*
expression, partly gratitude, partly fear, and sketches a goodbye with his arm.
SHAMHAT *exits with the* MAJOR-DOMO. ENKIDU *lies back,*
exhausted, and the room gradually grows dark. Silence and stillness for a while.
Then ENKIDU *begins to move about restlessly on the bed, sighing and*
muttering, and evidently in the grip of some dream or nightmare. He sits up
abruptly with a shout.

ENKIDU
    Gilgamesh! Gilgamesh! Oh, where are you?

GILGAMESH, *who had been resting in the next room, hurries in, belting his*
robe.

GILGAMESH
    I am here, I am here. Nothing can harm you.

ENKIDU
    It is churning through me, it is burning, the worm,
    the demon, in my bowels, like a storm
    of blood. But worse still is the deadly dream
    I never had till now. Oh it would seem
    that heaven cried out and earth replied, and I
    stood helplessly between. I too gave a cry
    as a dark face loomed up, terrifying,
    a lion-man, a lion-eagle flying
    from distant world to world, his hands were paws,
    his nails were talons, my hair in his claws,
    he overpowered me but I hit him hard,
    he jumped back like a dancer, broke my guard,
    struck and half-felled me, fully felled me,
    stamped on me like a wild bull, held me

clamped hideously at last, body to body.
I cried for help, to you, to anybody,
but neither you nor anyone came near.
The worst thing came, the very oldest fear.

ENKIDU *is shaken by a shivering fit, but struggles to continue.*

GILGAMESH
Tell me what I do not want to hear.

ENKIDU
He then prepared me for another sphere.
He feathered my arms like wings, he gripped me tight,
he led me down into the House of Night,
the House where those who enter do not come out,
the road of no return winds them about,
the House where those who live there have no light,
eat clay, sup mud, and though there is no flight
are clothed with feathers, stalking round like birds,
looking for the no light they stalk towards.
The door and the lock of that House are dust-encrusted.
It is the House of Dust, where zombies are mustered.
All round I saw piles of crowns like skulls.
All round I heard dead kings like kitchen trulls
shuffle to serve the gods with meats and sweetmeats
or pour thin skins of water at their seats.
In the House of Dust I saw where the high priest sits
with acolytes, exorcists, evangelists
and all the anointed priests of the pantheon.
I saw Ereshkigal, Underworld Queen,
seated there with Beletseri, Underworld Scribe,
kneeling before her and reading out the tribe
of the dying and the dead. She lifted up her head
when she saw me. 'Who brought him?' she said.

GILGAMESH
Is that not a good omen, that you went
only in dream, and that death is not meant?

ENKIDU *is racked with a fit of coughing, straining himself to resume.*

ENKIDU
What is there left of this body to save?
How easily it will slip into the grave!

To think of all the life I might have led
oh what an end, crippled on a bed –
they say to die in battle is the best –
but surely I might somehow have been blest
if I had died in the dangerous wilderness
when we were fighting monsters. Less and less
my honour seems. Where are the great trees
I ravaged for a paltry gate? The keys
of drunken guards are fumbled in the locks.
For this I left my forests and my flocks?
Bear with me, Gilgamesh. Help me. Hold me.
Oh how I need the bond of love to enfold me!
– It has come. I cannot see, or feel.
Now I shall know whether the dream was real.

ENKIDU's *death-rattle tells* GILGAMESH *it is all over. He tries his heart
but there is no beat. He closes the staring, sightless eyes. He draws the white
sheet up over* ENKIDU's *head. He stands up, utters a loud cry, and tears his
robe from top to bottom.*

GILGAMESH
Enkidu! What shall I do without my brother?
I have no other, never will have another!

Scene Three

Three days later. A room in the palace, hung with black. The coffin of
ENKIDU, *made of that same cedarwood the obtaining of which had such
tragic consequences, stands midstage on a catafalque, guarded by two soldiers,
one at each end, armed, with heads bowed.* GILGAMESH *lies prostrate on the
floor. Strong light on coffin and actors. This is held for a few seconds, like a
tableau. Then* GILGAMESH *gets to his feet. He is unkempt and still wears
his torn robe.*

THE LAMENT OF GILGAMESH OVER ENKIDU

Enkidu in your box of cedar, may the roads to the Cedar Forest
    be loud in mourning for you.
May the elders of great-walled broad-spread Uruk go clamorously
    mourning for you.

May the nomads roaming on hills and mountains remember you and
    walk in fond mourning for you.
May the ploughed fields, as if they were your mother, cry out
    in fruitless mourning for you.
May cypress and pine, and even the cedar we attacked in our foray,
    shake in heavy mourning for you.
May panther and tiger, bear and buffalo, jackal and hyena, lion and
    bull, ibex and stag, and all the beasts of the Sumerian
    plains, run angrily mourning for you.
May the pure Euphrates where we used to fill our water-skins
    ripple its mourning for you.
May the citizens who watched us kill the Bull of Heaven be in
    trembling mourning for you.
May the farmer in whose song your name was inserted work on in
    mourning for you.
May the workers who produced butter and beer for you go darkly
    mourning for you.
May the harlot who massaged you with oil till you were very happy
    go weepingly in mourning for you.
May even the paid mourners with their shaven heads step genuinely
    mourning for you.
Enkidu, your mother the gazelle
and your father the wild donkey
and the wild asses who weaned you
and the herds who taught you fieldcraft
lie in the wastelands of forgetfulness.
But I am all memory, I
shriek for you like a mother.
I veiled your face like a bride's.
swooped over you like an eagle,
prowled about like a lioness
whose cubs have been snatched from her.
You were the axe at my side,
you were the sword at my waist,
you were the sash at my thighs
till a demon swept that away.
My friend, swift mule, wild ass,
my panther of the wilderness,
Enkidu, swift mule, wild ass,
my panther of the wilderness,
who went with me to the mountains
and with me destroyed Humbaba
and with me the Bull of Heaven,
you are dark in sleep, and your ears

are deaf to my lament.
Earth, hear my lament.

GILGAMESH *throws himself prostrate as he was at the beginning of the scene.*

Scene Four

The market-place at Uruk. Funeral procession across stage with ENKIDU*'s coffin. Fronds of greenery, and a golden crown, have been placed on the coffin lid. Wild, harsh music. Despite* ENKIDU*'s regrets about dying unheroically in bed, with a mysterious sickness, it is soldiers who carry the coffin. Citizens line the street, silent, sad, respectful.* GILGAMESH *leads the mourners following the coffin, and in the procession we can pick out* SHAMHAT, NEDU, *the* JESTER, NINSUN, *and the* MAJOR-DOMO. *From her temple wall,* ISHTAR *surveys the scene with an expression of satisfaction. Having got* ENKIDU *out of the way, she feels that this is at least a good act of vengeance against* GILGAMESH. *After the cortège has passed, but before the citizens disperse, a* SINGER *stands out from the crowd and delivers the*

SONG OF THE DEATH OF YOUNG MEN

Some are brought back from battles.
The body-bags lie in rows.
Some die at the high passes,
shrouded only in snows.

Sailors never returning
kick-box unbeatable deeps.
Homeless youths in winter
stiffen in the streets.

Strength and beauty vanish
as if they had never been.
They live in this dimension
where love is evergreen.

And love is green for ever
when we sing them to their rest.
But they cut the rest to tatters
and spike the grieving breast.

75

Scene Five

A room in the palace. GILGAMESH *and his mother* NINSUN *are sitting talking.*

GILGAMESH
  I have to go. There is nothing for me here.
  My memories are too terrible, too near.
  I have signed my last decree, for craft and art –
  my blacksmiths, lapidaries, sculptors, jewellers – to start
  making a statue of Enkidu, with lapis-lazuli,
  for the chest where his rich heart used to be,
  and a body of gold untarnishably bright.
  It will be a landmark, more than human height.
  But me: I shall dress myself in skins
  and roam the wilderness. Caravans, inns,
  camp-fires I shall neither seek nor reject.
  What comfort, what solace can I now expect?

NINSUN
  My son, you must expect something. Why go?

GILGAMESH
  Why go? Oh mother, I am afraid of what I know.
  I am going to die. Enkidu tells me that.
  For forty, fifty years we might have sat
  together and ruled Uruk. I was learning,
  I was beginning. That power needs earning
  he told me, he showed me. I truly was beginning
  to see that there was something more worth the winning
  than what I had. All that has gone since he is gone.
  I have lost my prop, my goad, my conscience. Brawn
  and gold chains are nothing. I am bound for death.
  But now I give myself, till my last breath,
  a search for the enemy of death. For there must be,
  beyond those sands and bones and misery,
  some immortality.

NINSUN
                    You want to try
  the Underworld, eat dust, sprout feathers, fly?

GILGAMESH
  These are priests' fables, told to frighten us.

NINSUN

You think there's something better? Enlighten us.

GILGAMESH

I have heard that there is an immortal man
who survived the Flood, under whatever plan
those ancient angry gods had scrambled and devised
to humiliate human kind. They tyrannised
the world from some incomprehensible pique,
some childish godly *realpolitik*,
and drowned the lot. The one left high and dry –
just as incomprehensibly, his tie
was neat, his incense was stronger, who knows –
received eternal life. He will disclose
his secret to me. I will track him down
from land to land. His secret did not drown
and I must have it. I cannot bear to die.

NINSUN

My son, the chariot rolls near, rolls by
and takes you with it. There is no other fate.

GILGAMESH

Man makes fate. Kings make fate. It is too late
to talk me out of it, mother. I am as ready
as I will ever be, my mind as steady,
to risk the unknown for a prize so precious.
I give up all these rooms, this fraud, these pleasures.
I am a crownless pilgrim and a wanderer.
Deserts and mountain winds, rough provender
are mine until I meet the man they say
is called Ziusura, Ziusura the Faraway.

NINSUN

You will not find him! You will not come back!

GILGAMESH

I will come back, even if the heavens crack.

They embrace, NINSUN *clinging to* GILGAMESH *even as he tries to pull
away.*

END OF ACT FOUR

Act Five
Scene One

*A wilderness. Wind blowing. Mountains looming up in background, with a
narrow pass leading into them. Frightening sounds as if from some alien
creatures. GILGAMESH enters, forcing his way against the wind. He is
dressed in rough animal skins and carries a staff and a pack; a dagger and an
axe are in his belt. Suddenly a SCORPION-MAN and his mate a
SCORPION-WOMAN jump into view and bar his path. These are the
guardians of the pass through the mountains. The wind calms down a bit while
they are speaking.*

SCORPION-MAN

Who is this? Who are you and why are you here?

SCORPION-WOMAN

You have come from afar. I can smell your fear.

SCORPION-MAN

Few travellers come – and we like it that way –
to enter the black mountains.

SCORPION-WOMAN

                            Night and day
we wait to raise our tails at vagabonds,
ruffians, gatecrashers. Once it responds,
our poison is unusually slow,
so if you want to suffer, let us know.

SCORPION-MAN

A bit of a god? A bit of a man? You're bold,
I admit that. We are scary, eh? All told,
you should explain yourself, and I mean now.

They give a little dance, with hissing, rattling sounds; very menacing.

GILGAMESH

I am Gilgamesh of Uruk. I have made a vow
to search for answers about life and death.
At the ends of the earth, with my last breath,
if I do not find immortality, I have failed.
I can never rest until I have hailed

Ziusura the Faraway, who survived the Flood,
and asked him what elixir fires his blood
to make him eternal.

SCORPION-MAN
                      No man has done that,
no man has been there, not since Ararat.
Who will guide you through the mountain passes?
Light is not given to the one who trespasses
among the hills that hide the eastern sun.
It is still day, but think when day is done
you are in pitch blackness – you stumble – you run –
demon voices ring out one by one –
now hot, now cold, the dusty wind will howl –

SCORPION-WOMAN
Your face will feel the feathers of the owl –

SCORPION-MAN
Will you go on, you king, you man, you seeker?

SCORPION-WOMAN
Can you be stronger when you are weaker?

GILGAMESH
I can be stronger when I am weaker.
Ziusura is the Faraway; I am the seeker.
I have not come this distance to turn back.
I am set, I am driven, show me the track.

SCORPION-MAN
Gilgamesh, I do not know what you will find.
You must follow the signposts of your mind.
We shall not interrupt your resolution.

SCORPION-WOMAN
Go forward. We are real, but there's illusion
ahead of you. You will be tested. Be too the tester.
Don't overplay the passion of the quester.

GILGAMESH
How could I overplay eternal life?

SCORPION-WOMAN
Sometimes we cut the knot, sometimes the knife.

With this riddling reply, SCORPION-MAN *and* SCORPION-WOMAN
scuttle and leap out of GILGAMESH's *path, and vanish. The wind picks up
again, and it grows dark, as* GILGAMESH *sets out on his journey through the
mountains. The mountain range is black against the dark blue sky, and the
range slowly moves from right to left as* GILGAMESH *pushes forward from
left to right, to indicate his progress. The moon appears from a bank of clouds,
and the moonlight shines on* GILGAMESH's *dagger, which he has drawn
from his belt in case of attack. Apart from that, the scene is dark. The wind
comes in gusts, interspersed with whirring and howling noises. And as the*
SCORPION-WOMAN *had foretold,* GILGAMESH's *head is buffeted by
the flapping wings of half-seen birds. He moves on as steadily as he can,
through this nightmare, and gradually the stage begins to lighten; the night is
over; he leaves the mountains for a more open landscape. As the sun comes up,
he finds himself entering a beautiful and brilliant garden, but it is an inorganic
garden, and something warns him to pass through it but not to linger. The trees
are made of precious stones. Trunks and branches, leaves and fruit are all
glittering jewels: lapis-lazuli and carnelian, ruby and emerald. Even thorns
and briars are flashing with red and blue and green. It is all artifice, like a
window-display at Aspreys, and* GILGAMESH *quickly realises that he
cannot pluck any of the fruit to slake his thirst. He moves admiringly from tree
to tree, but shakes his head as he touches the stone-hard branches and foliage.
As he leaves the garden, he hears the sound of waves breaking on a shore, and
seagulls. He hurries in their direction.*

Scene Two

*A tavern by the edge of the sea. A small wood is beside it. In the bay is a
catamaran of tied and tarred logs. The tavern door is closed, and* SIDURI, *the
female tavern-keeper, is inside, looking out of the window at the unkempt and
travel-weary figure of* GILGAMESH *as he draws near. He is still holding the
dagger, and she is alarmed at what she sees as a threatening visitor. She bolts
the lock of the door with a bang, and returns to the window.*

SIDURI
      Don't come any closer! We're not open yet.
      We don't do breakfast anyway, so *get!*
      Tramps and beggars, murderers, the lot –
      everyone thinks this is a remote spot
      where pickings are easy. I've got a friend
      (*dog barks fiercely*)

with teeth, I've got a knife, and I can fend,
oh I can fend. My takings are well stashed.
And I made *him* sorry, one that flashed.
(*Coarse laugh and gesture*)
So what the hell d'you want?

GILGAMESH (*hurriedly puts dagger back in belt*)
                    Madam –

SIDURI
                              Siduri.

GILGAMESH
    Madam Siduri –

SIDURI

                    Just Siduri.

GILGAMESH
                    Your fury
is misplaced. Not an ounce of bad intent
is in me. I am King Gilgamesh. I went
out from Uruk on a great search –

SIDURI
                                        Uruk?
A king? In skins? That lets you off the hook?
You're filthy, you're hardly decent. I have a man
sweeps out the yard who's from a better clan.

GILGAMESH (*begins to get exasperated*)
    No you have not, Siduri. A long line
of thrones and powers reaching back to the divine
is mine. If you must judge by what you see,
see this.

*He comes nearer to the tavern, takes off his gold ring with the royal seal and
holds it out towards her. Against her will she examines it, and is half-satisfied,
but doubts remain.*

SIDURI
        The royal seal? Why should you be
roaming like an animal through the wilderness?

81

GILGAMESH (*getting angry*)
Siduri, I have smashed down doors for less!
I am Gilgamesh, and what I do I do.
I have killed lions with my hands. I slew
the Guardian of the Cedar Forest. I downed
the Bull of Heaven, made him smell death.

SIDURI
                                        Crowned
king, you say? Strangler of lions? Executioner
of wood demons, divine bulls? Elocutioner,
tall-tale teller are you? Why, if it is true,
is your face so thin and haggard? Who drew
sleepless circles under your eyes? How come
you look as if you'd trudge till kingdom come,
through ice and heat, like a camp-follower
without a camp?

GILGAMESH
                        Tavern-keeper, the flower
of youth, my friend and brother Enkidu,
sharer of many dangers we came through,
co-striker at Humbaba and the Bull,
my friend who shared all hardship to the full
and whom I deeply love, Enkidu who
shared all that hardship to the full, who knew
I deeply loved him, has served the general fate
of men. I mourned him, desolate,
letting no one bury him till the worm
crawled from his nose. I was unclean, infirm,
terrified, dying! I would follow him,
how could I escape? The worm was so grim,
the face was so dreadful, I tore my robes,
I cried, I began to roam long roads.
How could I be silent, how could I be still?
He is clay, the friend I love. What skill,
what search, what secret can save me from the clay?

SIDURI *is persuaded at last by* GILGAMESH*'s eloquence.*

SIDURI
Well, Gilgamesh the King, I hear what you say.
You are man, you have suffered, you are driven.
You may get a dry answer from heaven,

82

for I think we all die. But if I can do
anything to help, I will.

GILGAMESH
Siduri, you
must have heard many travellers, many rumours.
You must have wheedled stories from your roomers.
How can I find Ziusura the Faraway?

SIDURI
First you must cross sea, by night, by day,
many miles, trackless waters, chill the blood,
no one has ever crossed there since the Flood,
except –

GILGAMESH
– except? –

SIDURI
Ziusura's ferryman,
whose job it is to pole his catamaran
out from this bay and keep the sea-lanes clear.
Even with him there's danger and there's fear.
His name is Urshanabi, he's over there
in the wood, with his lodestones, take care
of the stones, that's how the boat is sped
through everything right to the Waters of the Dead.
Speak to him – he can help – he can show –
But wait – before you go – if you must go –
you need to take some food and drink –

SIDURI *disappears from the window, and in a moment or so she opens the door
and hands a package to* GILGAMESH. *He hurries towards the copse, dagger
and axe in his hands, suddenly aggressive and domineering again.*

GILGAMESH
Lodestones?
No thanks, I want to sail with flesh and bones.
Let Urshanabi keep his mumbo-jumbo –
or rather let him not. I'll make a gumbo
of his bloody lodestones. Urshanabi!
Gilgamesh is here. Let's see your scabby
magic!

83

URSHANABI, *the strapping young ferryman, appears in the wood and watches in angry amazement as* GILGAMESH *lays about him with his axe and smashes the lodestones.*

I've spooked your stones, don't try to tout them!

URSHANABI
You fool, how can we navigate without them?

They fight over the stones. Neither wins. They stand apart, panting.
GILGAMESH, *as we know, is a man of moods, and his outburst evaporates quickly.* URSHANABI *adjusts.*

URSHANABI
Gilgamesh, we now have an engineless ferry,
do you hear me, a non-magnetic wherry.
It suits the job: here is a king in tatters,
itching to broach improbably high matters
with my improbable master, Ziusura.
There isn't any chapter, verse, or sura
I'm sure he couldn't quote and say 'Discuss!'
He is the Faraway, but he draws us
even without a lodestone. Are we strong then?
What are we in the field and lot of men?
If you are not afraid to be a wood-cutter
once more, we'll make some oars to get this cutter
going – oars, punt-poles, masts, whatever,
for deeps or shallows, doldrums or wild weather.
You could be fishing for a final cast!
The lubber king will serve before the mast
or even be the mast! Go take your axe,
cut down some young and springy trees; quick hacks,
rough work will do; time presses; then to the boat.

GILGAMESH *obediently goes with his axe into the wood. Sounds of chopping, slicing, thudding. He reappears with an armful of poles, which he and* URSHANABI *load onto the flat, sail-less catamaran. Standing on the ferry, they row or pole themselves out from the shore.* SIDURI *watches them for a moment, then goes into the tavern.*

GILGAMESH (*distant voice*)
Urshanabi, at least we are afloat!
The other shore – how far is it ahead?

URSHANABI (*distant voice*)
  What is time? These are the Waters of the Dead.

Gradual darkness as they glide away into the distance. The sea is calm.

Scene Three

Rough sea. Wind gusting. The ferry is at the last stage of the voyage, making for Ziusura's shore.

URSHANABI (*loudly, against the wind*)
  Gilgamesh, we need a sail! Take off your pelt!
  Make a mast of a punt-pole, use your belt!
  Take off your skins!

GILGAMESH
                    Take off my skin? You think
  I'm a snake?

URSHANABI
            Skins, skins! Otherwise we'll sink!

GILGAMESH *undoes his belt, takes off his garment of skins, buckles himself to a pole, and stands with his arms spread holding the pelt like a sail. The boat catches the wind and is soon driven onto the shore. The two men disembark, and* URSHANABI *ties up the boat.* GILGAMESH *puts on his pelt again. While* URSHANABI *is attending to the ferry, examining it, tightening up its thongs, etc.,* GILGAMESH *leaves him and walks off to the nearest house, which is* ZIUSURA's, *though* GILGAMESH *does not know this yet. A well set up, impressive-looking man in his forties, dressed casually but comfortably in a style different from the styles of Uruk, comes out to meet him.* GILGAMESH *at first fails to recognise that this is the very man he seeks,* ZIUSURA, *since the mental image he had was of some Swiftian Struldbrug several centuries old, and he does not realise that* ZIUSURA *had been allowed to retain his age at the time when he and his family were saved from the Flood. Although* ZIUSURA *and his people behave like ordinary human beings, there should be a certain indefinable strangeness (perhaps done through lighting) about his house and the town behind it, since they exist, after all, beyond the Waters of the Dead.*

ZIUSURA (*polite but puzzled*)
  Sir, you are not one of our people, surely,
  although your boat sailed in and beached securely.
  Your boat, *our* boat. But where are its lodestones?
  You improvised a sail. I sense – overtones –
  something I do not understand. I ask,
  in courtesy, what is your mission, your task?
  And why are you so travel-stained and haggard?

GILGAMESH
  Sir, I have sailed and hunted, struggled, staggered
  through seas and mountains, deserts, pseudo-gardens
  and real forests, chasing and chased by guardians
  of darkest places, searching till my last breath
  how I might slip the hunter's noose of death.
  I am King Gilgamesh who buried his friend
  Enkidu at the very other end
  of the world, and now I cannot stop or stay
  till I have found Ziusura the Faraway
  who holds the secret of life undying.

ZIUSURA
                              Why,
  Gilgamesh, do you scour earth, sea, and sky –
  and even what is beyond sky, earth, and sea –
  since the Waters of the Dead brought you to me –
  in search of – what? Some smiling holy fool,
  some dunghill guru, some gap-toothed Gagool?
  You unkinged yourself, you disrobed – look at you –
  for what?

GILGAMESH
            I suffered –

ZIUSURA
                  You suffered, he suffered too,
  we suffered, they suffered, a whole conjugation
  suffered, as she did, your mother, and your nation.
  What good did sackcloth and ashes ever do?

GILGAMESH
  They told the world how I loved Enkidu.

86

ZIUSURA
Enkidu, Enkidu! You blow on one reed.
He cannot be freed, but others can be freed.
The gods may want you to take care, take heed
of something different from your own dark need.

GILGAMESH
My need is terrible. I am broken. I need life.

ZIUSURA
We all need life, but then there comes a knife.
We need a life, but then we get a death.
It stalks us with its old insidious breath.
No one can see it, no one sees its face.
Its savage grimace has no shape, no grace.
How long do we think home and hearth will last?
How long will the sealed document be passed?
How long do brothers share their inheritance?
How long will rivers rise and swell to the dance
of dragonflies with their eyes turned to the sun?
But no one really sees the sun, not one.
The sleeping and the dead are but as pictures,
but death is not a picture; divine strictures
make dreadful secrets better secret. The day
of its coming, even to Ziusura the Faraway,
is hidden.

GILGAMESH
            You are Ziusura, are you not?

ZIUSURA
I am.

GILGAMESH
        You are a dragonfly of thought
above a river of feeling. My mind spins.

ZIUSURA
The sun is well up now, and the mist thins.
Come to my house. We'll eat, and talk.

ZIUSURA *leads the way towards the door of his house.*

Scene Four

A room in Ziusura's house. Table set for a simple meal, which ZIUSURA'S
WIFE *is preparing and then bringing to the table. She is a kindly, bustling
woman, and (as with her husband) she looks a well-preserved forty rather than
the hundreds (or more likely thousands) of years she has actually lived. Such
furnishings as the room has should be simple, but with that slight element of
difference or strangeness already mentioned in connection with the external
appearance of the house and town. Perhaps again a lighting effect will do the
trick.*

ZIUSURA'S WIFE (*offering food to* GILGAMESH *as he sits at the table*)
                      Gilgamesh,
  you must eat. The sea is cold to human flesh,
  the Waters of the Dead are even colder.
  Your lion-skin is thin upon your shoulder.
  We shall find you things to wear. In the meantime,
  warm yourself with this right fiery wine!

GILGAMESH (*drinks*)
  Excellent! Is this vintage from before the Flood
  or after? (*He laughs*)

ZIUSURA'S WIFE
  Ah, you may laugh, but there's not one taste bud
  could believe the count of years. We have means
  of preservation that would haunt your dreams.

GILGAMESH
  You two are the best advertisement for that.
  Is it the air, is it the habitat,
  some divine regimen, or genes, or diet?
  Could Uruk, wealthiest of the cities, buy it?
  Is it truly what I came these miles to find,
  eternal life that might assuage a mind
  corroded by the cries from vanished clay?

ZIUSURA
  Gilgamesh, let me fill your glass. Today –

ZIUSURA'S WIFE
  Before you start, another slice? –

GILGAMESH

                              It is good,
thank you.

ZIUSURA

          Thank you my dear.

GILGAMESH

                        You still eat food –
forgive my rudeness – your metabolism –

ZIUSURA

      – is human. Cells renew. There is no ageism.

GILGAMESH

      And you and your wife – do you still – ?

ZIUSURA'S WIFE (*laughs*)

                            Gilgamesh!
You want to see some ivy-mouldered crèche?
We are not dead. We are not sick. We live.

GILGAMESH

      And memory – ?

ZIUSURA

               – is sharp, as I shall give
you proof of. You came here with your bereavement.
You knew too well, too long, what human grief meant.
Why do men die? Do all men die? Shall I?
You sought to force the fountainhead, the one
who had survived everything under the sun
for let us say more than a millennium –

ZIUSURA'S WIFE

      – or two – or three –

ZIUSURA

                  I could do the sum
but it would not be meaningful to you.
Today, though, you will hear my story, true
as I can tell it. When the earth was young –
and there were more people then than now – some tongue
began to wag in heaven about our faults –

we were too many, too noisy, frisky as colts,
proud, irreverent, God knows what else – so
we must be taught a lesson – do you know
the world is mostly water?

GILGAMESH
                    Surely not!

ZIUSURA
Ah but it is. God, Anu, whoever, shot
such a flood from the sky that almost the land
disappeared, and people with it. Like a hand
with kittens in a pail, vengeance was taken.
I must have had friends in heaven, shaken
by pity. Voices told me to build a boat
enormous, solid, well-caulked to float
but high and square like an ocean ziggurat
and filled with my family and friends who sat
or stood under the battened deck. My God
we used gallons of bitumen! Silver and gold
were stowed in chestfuls. A party for the workmen,
beer and wine like river water. The watermen
banged the rollers and jumped aboard. We were off.
Oh Gilgamesh, a storm not to be thought of
raged round the earth that day, and seven days.
The air was black, the ocean swelled, a blaze
of lightning-bolts on burning buildings showed
those who ran smouldering to be drowned. Every road
vanished, the earth shattered like a pot.
We drove out, safely timbered. The sea fought
the land and laid it so low it was not to be seen.
After a week the air turned calm and serene.
I opened a hatch, a fresh breeze touched my cheek.
Nothing was living, you could seek and seek
but only the wet expanse flat as a roof
rolled above the dead. If they wanted proof,
those gods, of their power, it weltered in the light.
I fell to my knees in that place at that sight,
and the tears streamed down my face.

GILGAMESH
                    You alone survived?

ZIUSURA
My boat, my wife, my workmen, my beasts arrived

at the only mountain-top that was still uncovered.
We disembarked, we stretched, we sang, we recovered.
The waters sank. I have lived since then,
and I have powers not given to other men.

GILGAMESH
The gods were good to you.

ZIUSURA
It is not good
to kill a million in a petulant mood.
The faces of the drowned can still accuse me.
It is for some horrible kudos the gods use me.

GILGAMESH
They created the world.

ZIUSURA
Did they so?
Who told us that, and why? How do we know?
Priests, temples, crumbling tablets, sacred rites?
Who, or what, divided the days and the nights?

GILGAMESH
These thoughts are on the edge.

ZIUSURA
So are we all,
but it is the edge of a mighty waterfall.

GILGAMESH
So can you give me immortality?

ZIUSURA (*laughs*)
Not quite like that. Have you the quality,
the potential, the strength? I have to test you,
and only if you pass can I divest you
of decay. You must sit there against the wall,
your head between your knees, not moving at all,
or lying down, or sleeping, the whole night through.
Let me see what you are made of.

GILGAMESH *sits hunched against the wall of the room, with his head bowed,
trying desperately to keep awake. But the combination of his tiredness after the*

91

*journey, and the wine he has drunk, defeats him, and he falls asleep, and even
snores. ZIUSURA and his WIFE watch him closely during these struggles.*

ZIUSURA'S WIFE
                              Ah, he's through.
Poor man. You are too hard on him, my dear.
Touch him awake. We must make it clear
he is to go home safely and without blame.
He could have done no more. I think his name
is not to be forgotten.

ZIUSURA
                              A little taunting
is in order, don't you feel? To be found wanting
at the most crucial moment of your quest –
yes yes I know, he's wearied and he's stressed –
but heroes – and he's surely one – should keep
fathoms of energy to scupper sleep.
Gilgamesh! (*He shakes him awake*) Gilgamesh, where have you been?
Eternal life has come and gone unseen.
Where is the lion, the great hunter, now?
Where are the conscious lightnings of his brow?
I cannot help you; you have failed the test.
You must go back; to go homewards is best.

GILGAMESH (*anguished*)
Oh Ziusura, what is to become of me?
What shall I do, by either land or sea?
The Raptor has sunk his claws into my flesh.
Death has squatted in the rooms of Gilgamesh.
Wherever I go, there already is Death!

ZIUSURA
Midnight comes; kings are clay; men are earth.
Great souls can live with a *memento mori*,
as the Hittites say. You will carry your story,
if not your life, across uncounted years
like an eagle in the universe. Your fears,
your tears are twigs in an unfinished nest.
What more? What else? It's beating in your breast!

GILGAMESH *gathers his things and prepares to leave.* ZIUSURA *calls
loudly for the ferryman.* URSHANABI *enters.*

ZIUSURA

Urshanabi, I do not need you here.
Gilgamesh is leaving. Take off his grimy gear,
let the sea sweep it away. At the washing-place
let him wash his matted hair, anoint his face
and body with fine oil, let his beautiful skin
be revived. See to it thoroughly. Bring in
fresh robes, fresh headband, laundered, royal.
On this journey they will not crease or soil,
such power I shall give them. Do it now.

URSHANABI *and* GILGAMESH *exeunt.*

ZIUSURA'S WIFE

Gilgamesh came to us in rags, God knows how.
His deepest hopes seem to have been disbanded.
We cannot let him go home empty-handed.

ZIUSURA

You don't think his new robes will be enough?
Uruk will marvel at such mystic stuff –
bandbox-pristine as he arrives, not a spot,
not a tear, a king reborn? Well, perhaps not.
You think some object, some material thing?

ZIUSURA'S WIFE

Something more impressive than a ring,
more useful than a nail from the boat of the Flood –

ZIUSURA

I know, I have it, something for the blood,
rejuvenation, a present for the old,
not immortality, but make them bold,
active, a second life, a second chance,
a second spring, a springboard and a dance –

ZIUSURA'S WIFE

You are very lyrical, but what is it?

ZIUSURA (*shouts outside*)

Gilgamesh! Urshanabi! (*To wife*) He will bless his visit.
Are you ready? Come in. Let me see you. Right!
Nothing will undo that splendid white.

GILGAMESH *and* URSHANABI *enter.* GILGAMESH *is transformed by his new clothes, which should be mainly white, to emphasise the wonder of their unsoilability.*

ZIUSURA

Gilgamesh, before you leave, go to the yard.
Plunge your arm into the well, hold hard
to a plant you will find growing there –
it has thorns like a rose, so take care –
and let me see you have it – as a gift
to Uruk. This is the plant that can lift
cowering old age to youth again. Use it well.

GILGAMESH *exits.* ZIUSURA *and his* WIFE *and* URSHANABI *talk quietly together, perhaps looking at map of the journey.* GILGAMESH *re-enters, holding the plant.*

GILGAMESH

It has a very subtle, pungent smell.
I never saw its like. All the old men
of Uruk shall taste it, and be born again.
I shall distil its essence, and I too
when I am grey will drink it and be new.

ZIUSURA

Be off then. Each look after the other.
Gilgamesh, Urshanabi is your brother.
Go overland this time. He knows the way.

GILGAMESH

Goodbye. Live well, Ziusura the Faraway.

ZIUSURA *and his* WIFE *stand watching as* GILGAMESH *and* URSHANABI *collect their travelling necessities and exeunt. They wave briefly.* ZIUSURA *and his* WIFE *wave back.*

Scene Five

A forest glade. Early evening. GILGAMESH *and* URSHANABI *have stopped for the night. They set down their packs,* GILGAMESH *carefully laying his plant on the ground.*

GILGAMESH
  A cosy place to stop, like a beast's lair.

URSHANABI
  We'll make a fire. Let's look for brushwood. There.

*They wander offstage, and shortly return with armfuls of brushwood. They
drop the brushwood in shock as they watch a large snake slither out of the trees,
snatch the plant in its jaws, and go back into the undergrowth. Before it
disappears, it sloughs its skin, to show a shining new body. The plant evidently
works, but it is gone for ever.* GILGAMESH *sits down, defeated, weeping.*

GILGAMESH
  Everything is lost now, Urshanabi!
  What comfort and what cost now, Urshanabi?
  Who have I laboured for with this arm?
  Who has my blood churned for? Oh what harm
  have I done instead of good: a beast
  has smacked its lips upon a human feast
  that might have been. I have nothing left.
  What shall I say to my city?

URSHANABI
                    A cleft
  rock may tremble, but still be home to seeds
  if you will let yourself grow into deeds.

URSHANABI *makes a fire. It grows dark.* GILGAMESH *sits staring into
the fire. It is hard to know whether he is at peace, but maybe he is beginning to
accept himself as he really is, and so be able to move on from there. Trees shown
in strong light from the fire.*

Scene Six

The market square in Uruk. Evening. It is more than a year since
GILGAMESH *left the city. The place is unchanged except for the large statue
of* ENKIDU, *in gold and lapis-lazuli, which has been erected near the great
cedar gate. News of* GILGAMESH's *imminent return has spread, and an
expectant public has filled the square.* NINSUN, GILGAMESH's *mother,
stands prominently at the gate, straining to catch sight of his approach. At last*

GILGAMESH *and* URSHANABI *appear,* URSHANABI *dusty and travel-stained,* GILGAMESH *still in his strangely unsullied robes.* NINSUN *runs to meet them, and clasps* GILGAMESH *with a cry.*

NINSUN
    My son, my son! is it really you at last?
    I hoped and hoped – but so much time has passed –
    are you well? – oh it is such a joy –

GILGAMESH
    Mother, I am safe, I am here. Nothing will destroy
    my love for the city I left, for you, for all.
    I have been far and learned much. The wall
    of Uruk, I see, still stands. Now I know wilderness
    and wall. If you ask how I have had to dress
    so white, so spotless, it is part of my long story
    which you shall hear in time. It has no glory
    but I shall tell it. This is my colleague
    and good friend, ferryman Urshanabi; league
    beyond league we sailed the Waters of the Dead.
    Now he will live in Uruk, and learn to tread
    hard ground instead of squelching logs.

URSHANABI
                        Madam,
    just watch my sea-legs pound the tarmacadam!
    I've had my fill of shark and hurricane.

GILGAMESH, URSHANABI *and* NINSUN *come right into the market square. People gather excitedly to hear what the returning, self-exiled king has to say.*

GILGAMESH
    My friends, you know I roamed the world in pain.
    Seas, deserts, monsters – oh I could fill
    a thousand tablets with an overkill
    of passion, danger, hopes dashed, black encounters.
    When I set out on those uncanny adventures
    I hardly thought I wanted to live, if living
    only led to dying. Forbidding, not forgiving
    seemed any gods or powers there might be.
    I sought Ziusura, who survived a sea
    that drowned the world of long ago, the Flood
    we still feel whispering through our blood

and build high walls and towers to forfend.
Ziusura has eternal life, and the end
of mine is like all men's, as I now know:
spade and shovel, down through sand or snow.
Immortality is a wilderness of fireflies
that dances to deceive our yearning eyes.
– And speaking of fireflies, let us have some light!
It grows dark in Uruk. Challenge the night!

Lamps and torches are lit throughout the square.

I cannot say I am an ordinary king.
I am not! But I have learned an ordinary thing:
whatever good can be done must be done here.
The Waters of the Dead howled in my ear
but could not deliver my gigantic dream.
I am among you, my exile is over, my scheme
of aggrandisement is in shards. I now proclaim
an amnesty of amnesties, and in my name,
soldiers, guards, open the prison gates,
let those I wronged come out, wipe all the slates,
heal the weals and wash off all the stains,
strike off the chains, dear god, strike off the chains!

Movement of soldiers and guards in background. Sound of chains. The
PRISONERS, *mostly young, of both sexes, stumble out, or preferably up, from
the state dungeons. Their chains are struck off. Bewildered at first, they soon
realise they are free, and begin to mingle with the crowd. There are recognition
scenes, families reunited, happy tears. It is now night in the city. Gradually the
whole movement of the crowd becomes a solemn dance. Music replaces the
voices. It swells, loud and thrilling, then slowly recedes. In the flickering light of
the torches, the dance slowly comes to a stop, and the now almost motionless
people are transformed into a thick, rustling mass of trees. Perhaps there is some
birdsong, as long as it is not overdone. Within this forest, light falls on the statue
of* ENKIDU, *its dead but living guardian.*

END OF ACT FIVE

END OF PLAY